DON'T WASTE YOUR LIFE

DON'T WASTE YOUR LIFE.

John Piper

STUDY GUIDE DEVELOPED BY DESIRING GOD

CROSSWAY
WHEATON, ILLINOIS

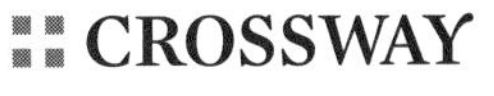

Don't Waste Your Life Study Guide

Published by Crossway
1300 Crescent Street
Wheaton, Illinois 60187

This study guide is based on and is a companion to *Don't Waste Your Life* by John Piper (Crossway Books, 2003).

Cover design: Matt Taylor

Cover photo: iStock

First printing, redesign, 2009

Printed in the United States of America

ISBN 13: 978-1-4335-0633-8

ISBN 10: 1-4335-0633-5

Crossway is a publishing ministry of Good News Publishers.

ML 20 19 18 17 16
15 14 13 12 11 10 9 8 7

CONTENTS

INTRODUCTION TO THIS STUDY GUIDE

A NEWLY RETIRED COUPLE moves to New Mexico to spend their twilight years on the golf course. A middle-aged man labors all day at the office to make enough money to provide his family with a nice house in a safe neighborhood and fun vacations in the summer. A young student enters college in hopes of gaining the education and skills needed to have a good career. Is this all there is to life? Or did God make us for something greater than the American Dream?

It is our conviction that God did indeed create us for more than the American Dream. Nevertheless, millions of people waste their lives in pursuit of the vain trappings of this world because they never discover the simple, obvious, glorious, biblical reality that "[God's] steadfast love is better than life" (Psalm 63:3). They are never gripped by the truth that "to live is Christ, and to die is gain" (Philippians 1:21). The awesome biblical promise that "the earth will be filled with the knowledge of the glory of the LORD as the waters cover the sea" (Habakkuk 2:14) has never landed on them by the power of the Holy Spirit and awakened them to a passion for God's supremacy in all things for the joy of all peoples through Jesus Christ.

Our prayer is that God would use this study guide to awaken in you a consuming desire to not throw your life away on "fatal success."[1] Our desire is that Jesus Christ would explode into your life, unite your fractured dreams and fragmented heart, and produce a single, holy, all-embracing passion for his name. And then our hope is that in this passion you would be set free from small dreams and weak visions, that you would lay down your life for the cause of Christ in the world. As Jesus said, "Whoever would save his life will lose it, but whoever loses his life for my sake and the gospel's will save it" (Mark 8:35).

This study guide is designed to be used in a ten-session,[2] guided group study that focuses on *Don't Waste Your Life* by John Piper.[3] Following an introductory lesson, each subsequent lesson examines one or two chapters in *Don't Waste Your Life*. The final lesson aims to sum up and synthesize the material that you've learned during the study.

Lesson 1 should be completed during the first group study session when you receive the book and the study guide. Lessons 2-9 are divided into four distinct parts: (1) five daily assignments taking you through the entirety of *Don't Waste Your Life*; (2) a section for further study entitled "Further Up and Further In" that allows you to probe more deeply into the material in each lesson; (3) a group activity that should be completed during the group study session; and (4) a homework activity that applies the lesson.

> Throughout this study guide, paragraphs printed in a shaded box (like this one) are excerpts from *Don't Waste Your Life* or other books written by John Piper or excerpts taken from

the *Desiring God* website (www.desiringGod.org). They are included to supplement the study questions, redirect your thinking, or summarize key points.

The daily workload is divided into five manageable assignments. Day 1 is a preparatory day in which important Scripture passages are examined, key concepts are introduced, and provocative questions are raised. This section should be completed *before* reading the assigned chapter.

Days 2-4 divide the particular chapter(s) into three sections. You should read the assigned pages in *Don't Waste Your Life* and then answer the questions. The questions will explore relevant Scripture passages, test your comprehension of the material, and encourage you to think critically about the truth being presented.

Day 5 is set aside for review and application. On this day you should review important parts of the chapter and highlight the truths, concepts, and ideas that were most meaningful to you. The questions on this day will also encourage you to apply what you have learned.

The section entitled "Further Up and Further In" provides you the opportunity to engage in further study of the material. You are encouraged to complete this section if you have time, as it will help you fully grasp the material. The next section in Lessons 2-9, entitled "Group Activity," should be completed when your small group meets each week. The final section, "Getting Practical," suggests one activity that you could begin to do the following week in order to live out the truth you've been learning.

Lesson 10 is designed to help you review, summarize, and synthesize what you have learned over the course of the study. Further instructions will be given when you reach that lesson.

Group leaders will want to read the Leader's Guide at the end of this study immediately.

Igniting a passion to make your life count is only possible by the grace of God. Therefore, we highly encourage you to pray as you work your way through this study guide. As you engage with the material each day, make it a habit to seek the blessing of the Lord in prayer. Pray that God would open your mind and your heart to see wonderful things in his Word. Pray that he would grant you the understanding and insight you need in order to apply what you learn to your life. Pray that God would cause you to rejoice in the truth. And pray that the group discussion each week will be mutually encouraging and edifying for all who are involved.

May God our Father grant you, by the power of the Holy Spirit, to see and savor the all-satisfying supremacy of Jesus Christ so that no one would say in the end, "I've wasted it!"

NOTES

1. This phrase is taken from *Don't Waste Your Life*, page 46.
2. While this study guide is ideally suited for a ten-session study, it is possible to complete it in five sessions. For instructions on how to use this study guide for a five-session group study, turn to Appendix A: A Five-Session Intensive Option.
3. This resource is designed to be used in a group setting. It can also be used, however, by an independent learner. Such a learner would have to determine for himself or herself how to use this resource in the most profitable way. If you can't join a group, consider starting one of your own!

LESSON 1

INTRODUCTION TO *DON'T WASTE YOUR LIFE*

LESSON OBJECTIVES

It is our prayer that after you have finished this lesson . . .

- You will have an idea of how you and others in your group view a wasted life.
- Your curiosity will be excited, and questions will begin to form.
- You will be eager to learn more about how you can avoid wasting your life.

ABOUT YOURSELF

1) What is your name?
2) Tell the group something significant about yourself that you would like them to know.
3) Describe your personal relationship with Jesus Christ.

A PREVIEW OF *DON'T WASTE YOUR LIFE*

1) In your mind, what is the difference between a wasted life and an unwasted life? How could you discern whether or not you are wasting your life?

Turn to the Contents page in *Don't Waste Your Life* and read the chapter titles.

2) Based on the titles of the chapters alone, which chapter(s) are you most looking forward to? Why does that chapter pique your interest?

Let one person read the Preface to *Don't Waste Your Life* (pages 9-10) aloud to the group.

On page 9 John Piper says the following:

> It was not always plain to me that pursuing God's glory would be virtually the same as pursuing my joy. Now I see that millions of people waste their lives because they think these paths are two and not one.

3) In your mind, is pursuing God's glory "virtually the same" as pursuing your joy? How do you conceive of these two pursuits? What do they have to do with wasting or not wasting your life?

LESSON 2

MY SEARCH FOR A SINGLE PASSION TO LIVE BY

A Companion Study to the Don't Waste Your Life, Chapter 1

LESSON OBJECTIVES

It is our prayer that after you have finished this lesson . . .

- You will have done some serious reflection on your life to this point and will have begun to look ahead to what God has for your future.
- You will have a better grasp of where true Meaning and Purpose can be found.
- You will be eager to learn more about how you can avoid wasting your life.

DAY 1—INITIAL QUESTIONS BEFORE YOU READ

No one sets out to waste his or her life. However, very few people actually give thought to how they can avoid wasting it. It seems that many people simply slide into whatever mold society and culture fashion for them. A person may start out seeking to "make life count" in a vague, fuzzy sort of way, but because he or she never gives any deep reflection to what exactly that means, the pains and pleasures of life squeeze out any aspirations to do something great and glorious with his or her life. The first two chapters of *Don't Waste Your Life* chronicle John Piper's early years in which he grappled greatly with what it would mean to not waste his life. In reading his story, our hope is that you would see the road he has traveled to arrive at his conclusions about the glory of God, the pursuit of joy, and the unwasted life.

+ **QUESTION 1:** Spend some time praying and reflecting on your life. How did you get to where you are today?[1]

› If you are in your teens or twenties, what dreams and plans do you have for your future?
› If you are middle-aged, how do you think you've lived thus far? What dreams and plans do you have for your future?
› If you are nearing retirement and beyond, how do you think you've lived your life? How do you hope to finish so that you can say in the end, "I didn't waste it"?

List three things you hope to accomplish by the end of your life. Be sure to include any Scripture verses that have been significant for you.

QUESTION 2: No matter how old we get, we always have questions about the deeper issues of life. What questions do you have about God, Purpose, Truth, Life, Death, or People? Record your "big" questions below.

DAY 2—ONLY WHAT'S DONE FOR CHRIST WILL LAST

Read from page 11 to the middle of page 14 in *Don't Waste Your Life* and answer the following questions.

QUESTION 3: On page 12 John Piper records one of his father's sermon illustrations that had a huge impact on him as a boy. What is your reaction to this illustration? Do you feel the same fear that John Piper did?

The plaque that hangs near John Piper's front door reads:

> Only one life,
> 'Twill soon be past;
> Only what's done
> for Christ will last.

Now read the words of the apostle Paul in Acts.

ACTS 20:24

But I do not account my life of any value nor as precious to myself, if only I may finish my course and the ministry that I received from the Lord Jesus, to testify to the gospel of the grace of God.

+ QUESTION 4: In light of this verse, is it true that "*only* what's done for Christ will last"? How important is the word "only"?

On page 13 John Piper says the following:

> What was the opposite of not wasting my life? "To be successful in a career"? Or "to be maximally happy"? Or "to accomplish something great"? Or "to find the deepest meaning and significance"? Or "to help as many people as possible"? Or "to serve Christ to the full"? Or "to glorify God in all I do"? Or was there a point, a focus, an essence to life that would fulfill every one of those dreams?

QUESTION 5: Give three answers to the question "What is the opposite of not wasting my life?" that a non-Christian might give. What, if anything, is defective about these answers?

DAY 3—BREATHING EXISTENTIALISM

Read from the middle of page 14 to the bottom of page 17 in *Don't Waste Your Life* and answer the following questions.

Existentialism is a philosophy that states, "Existence precedes essence." This means that there is no objective Essence, Meaning, Truth, or Purpose "out there" for us to seek and find. The only "essence" or "truth" that exists is the kind that *we* create. In other words, if we set out to pursue Meaning and Truth outside of ourselves, then, according to existentialism, we are like the two men in Samuel Beckett's play (page 15) who wait for Godot, who never comes. Existentialism says, "It is foolish to go looking for something (Meaning, Essence, Purpose) 'out there' that doesn't exist. Instead you should just create your own Meaning, your own Essence, your own Purpose, your own Truth."

Study Genesis 1:1 and John 1:1-3.

GENESIS 1:1

In the beginning, God created the heavens and the earth.

JOHN 1:1-3

[1] *In the beginning was the Word, and the Word was with God,*
and the Word was God. [2] *He was in the beginning with God.*
[3] *All things were made through him, and without him was not*
any thing made that was made.

+ **QUESTION 6:** According to these verses, who or what was "in the beginning," before any human being existed? How do these verses answer the claim of existentialism that human beings create their own truth and essence?

QUESTION 7: John Piper contrasts the Beatles song "Nowhere Man" with Bob Dylan's song "Blowin' in the Wind" (pages 15-17). When you read the lyrics of these two songs, what is the main difference that you notice between the viewpoints represented in them?

DAY 4—LEARNING THE OBVIOUS

Read from the top of page 18 through page 22 and answer the following questions.

QUESTION 8: In this chapter John Piper compares his years at college learning the obvious to a fish that goes to school to learn there is water (page 18). Reflect on your formative years in high school or college. Have you ever had to "learn the obvious"? Describe your journey in the space below.

+ **QUESTION 9:** Do you consider yourself to be

A) a more logical and rational person,

or

B) a more emotional and playful person?

In your experience are these mutually exclusive options? Should we *strive* to combine them? Defend your answer.

On page 19 John Piper says (regarding C.S. Lewis):

> He demonstrated for me and convinced me that rigorous, precise, penetrating logic is not opposed to deep, soul-stir-

> ring feeling and vivid, lively—even playful—imagination. He was a "romantic rationalist." He combined things that almost everybody today assumes are mutually exclusive: rationalism and poetry, cool logic and warm feeling, disciplined prose and free imagination.

+ **QUESTION 10:** Compare your answer from Question 9 to the following verses from the Bible.

1 CORINTHIANS 13:6

[Love] does not rejoice at wrongdoing, but rejoices with the truth.

JOHN 4:23-24

[23] *But the hour is coming, and is now here, when the true worshipers will worship the Father in spirit and truth, for the Father is seeking such people to worship him.* [24] *God is spirit, and those who worship him must worship in spirit and truth.*

MATTHEW 22:35-38

[35] *And one of them, a lawyer, asked him a question to test him.*
[36] *"Teacher, which is the great commandment in the Law?"*
[37] *And he said to him, You shall love the Lord your God with all your heart and with all your soul and with all your mind.*
[38] *This is the great and first commandment."*

How do these verses portray the relationship between head and heart, thinking and feeling? Underline phrases in these verses that address this question, and record your reflections below.

DAY 5—REVIEW AND APPLICATION

Review your answers from the previous four days and any parts of *Don't Waste Your Life* that you want and then answer the following questions.

+ **QUESTION 11:** What was the most meaningful part of this chapter for you? Was there a sentence, concept, or idea that really struck you? Why? Record your thoughts in the space below.

+ **QUESTION 12:** What questions, if any, do you have about the material covered in this chapter? Write them below, and bring them up in your small group time.

FURTHER UP AND FURTHER IN[2]

Study the following verses from Romans.

ROMANS 1:18-23

> [18] *For the wrath of God is revealed from heaven against all*
> *ungodliness and unrighteousness of men, who by their unrigh-*
> *teousness suppress the truth.* [19] *For what can be known about*
> *God is plain to them, because God has shown it to them.* [20] *For*
> *his invisible attributes, namely, his eternal power and divine*
> *nature, have been clearly perceived, ever since the creation of the*

> *world, in the things that have been made. So they are without excuse. [21] For although they knew God, they did not honor him as God or give thanks to him, but they became futile in their thinking, and their foolish hearts were darkened. [22] Claiming to be wise, they became fools, [23] and exchanged the glory of the immortal God for images resembling mortal man and birds and animals and reptiles.*

QUESTION 13: In this chapter John Piper recounted how he went to school to "learn the obvious." According to these verses, why is it obvious that there is "Truth" (with a capital T) in the world? Are men ignorant of Truth, or do they suppress Truth?

QUESTION 14: In your own words, restate the main point of Romans 1:18-23. How does this passage offer an explanation for the existence of different philosophies, religions, and worldviews that deny the existence of "the God Who Is There"?

Study the following verses from Exodus.

EXODUS 3:13-14

> *Then Moses said to God, "If I come to the people of Israel and say to them, 'The God of your fathers has sent me to you,' and they ask me, 'What is his name?' what shall I say to them?"*

> [14] *God said to Moses, "I AM WHO I AM." And he said, "Say this to the people of Israel, 'I AM has sent me to you.'"*

QUESTION 15: According to this passage, God's name is "I AM WHO I AM." How does this verse respond to those who say that there is no Reality (Meaning, Essence, Purpose) until we create it? Where is Ultimate Reality found?

> It is blasphemy to say that there is a higher reality than God to which he must conform in order to be holy. God is the absolute reality beyond which is only more of God. When asked for his name in Exodus 3:14 he said, "I am who I am." His being and his character are utterly undetermined by anything outside himself.[3]

GROUP ACTIVITY

Complete this section during the group time each week.

Break into small groups, and share a small portion of your story from Question 1.

GETTING PRACTICAL

A suggested activity to do in the future: Begin to pray for a coworker, friend, or family member who doesn't know Jesus. Pray that God would make his or her heart soft and receptive to the Gospel. Make it a regular practice to pray for this person. If you have a family, invite them to pray with you for this person.

NOTES

1. Questions marked with a cross (+) are questions that we deem to be particularly significant for group discussion. See the Leader's Guide for more information.
2. The phrase "further up and further in" is borrowed from C. S. Lewis.
3. Taken from http://www.desiringGOD.org/ResourceLibrary/Sermons/ByDate/1984/419_Holy_Holy_Holy_Is_The_Lord_of_Hosts/.

LESSON 3

BREAKTHROUGH—THE BEAUTY OF CHRIST, MY JOY

A Companion Study to Don't Waste Your Life, Chapter 2

LESSON OBJECTIVES

It is our prayer that after you have finished this lesson . . .

- You will understand that it is possible to discover the original intent of an author when you read a text.
- You will begin to see the relationship between God's glory and our joy.
- You will have begun to think hard about what it means to be loved by God and what it means to love others.

DAY 1—INITIAL QUESTIONS BEFORE YOU READ

This chapter will continue the story begun in Chapter 1. John Piper will describe how the search for Meaning and Essence and Purpose (in other words, the search for the unwasted life) came together for him. For John Piper, the end of his soul's quest for its purpose centered on his joy and the glory of God.

Blaise Pascal was a French mathematician who died in 1662. One of his most famous works was entitled *Pensées*. The following paragraph from that work had a profound influence on John Piper in his formative years.

> All men seek happiness. This is without exception. Whatever different means they employ, they all tend to this end. The cause of some going to war, and of others avoiding it, is the same desire in both, attended with different views. This is the motive of every action of every man, even of those who hang themselves.[1]

QUESTION 1: Is it true that all men seek happiness (even those who commit suicide)? Is the pursuit of happiness inevitable? How do you think the Bible regards the pursuit of happiness? Cite Scripture verses in your answer.

QUESTION 2: When you hear the phrase *the glory of God*, what comes to mind? What does the Bible mean by "the glory of God"?

QUESTION 3: How would you define or describe love? How does the world define or describe love?

DAY 2—DISCOVERING THE ORIGINAL MEANING

Read from page 23 to the bottom of page 28 in *Don't Waste Your Life* and answer the following questions.

In the first part of this chapter, John Piper recounts his years at seminary and his struggle to discover whether it was possible to understand what an author was originally trying to convey in the Bible (or any other text). There were (and are) those who insist that it is impossible to discover what an author (whether the apostle Paul or William Shakespeare) was trying to communicate in his words. In this view, when we read, all we can do is talk about our own personal, subjective impressions about the words on the page. But we cannot accurately discover what the author was originally saying.

QUESTION 4: Why do you think John Piper includes this section on whether it is legitimate to try and discover the author's meaning in the text? How do you think his calling to be a minister of the Word of God relates to his desire to know if we can have access to the original meaning the author intended?

DAY 3—THE GLORY OF GOD IN THE JOY OF MAN

Read from page 29 to the middle of page 34 in *Don't Waste Your Life* and answer the following questions.

In his 22nd Resolution, Jonathan Edwards states:

> Resolved, to endeavor to obtain for myself as much happiness, in the other world, as I possibly can, with all the power, might, vigor, and vehemence, yea violence, I am capable of, or can bring myself to exert, in any way that can be thought of.[2]

+ QUESTION 5: How would you respond to someone who said, in reference to the resolution above, "No Christian should talk like that; Christians are not supposed to be self-centered"?

But we have learned from the Bible (and from Edwards!) that God's interest is to magnify the fullness of His glory by spilling over in mercy to us. Therefore, the pursuit of our interest and our happiness is never *above* God's, but always *in* God's. The most precious truth in the Bible is that God's greatest interest is to glorify the wealth of His grace by making sinners happy in Him—in *Him*![3]

Study the following two passages.

ISAIAH 43:6-7

6 I will say to the north, Give up,
and to the south, Do not withhold;
bring my sons from afar
and my daughters from the end of the earth,
7 everyone who is called by my name
whom I created for my glory,
whom I formed and made.

1 CORINTHIANS 10:31

So, whether you eat or drink, or whatever you do, do all to the glory of God.

QUESTION 6: According to these verses, what was God's purpose in creating us? Why do we exist?

Study the following verse.

PSALM 34:3

Oh, magnify the LORD *with me, and let us exalt his name together!*

QUESTION 7: John Piper notes that "to glorify" something is virtually the same as "to magnify" it (page 32). Are we supposed to magnify God like a microscope or like a telescope? What is the difference?

DAY 4—THE CENTRALITY OF JESUS

Read from the bottom of page 34 through page 40 in *Don't Waste Your Life* and answer the following questions.

Imagine the following scenario:

You are eating dinner with a group of friends. Suddenly one of your friends stands up, looks around the room, and says, "I love you all very deeply. My deepest desire is that all of you in this room could be with me all the time. More than anything, I want all of you to be around me and see my greatness. O how I want all of you to experience how wonderful I am!"

+ QUESTION 8: If your friend said such a thing, would you feel loved by him? Why or why not?

Study the words of Jesus in John 17.

JOHN 17:24-26

[24] Father, I desire that they also, whom you have given me, may be with me where I am, to see my glory that you have given me because you loved me before the foundation of the world. [25] O righteous Father, even though the world does not know you, I know you, and these know that you have sent me. [26] I made known to them your name, and I will continue to make it known, that the love with which you have loved me may be in them, and I in them.

+ QUESTION 9: Is this prayer by Jesus an expression of his love? Do you feel loved by Jesus when he prays this for you? Does your answer to this question differ from your answer to Question 8? If so, why is there a difference?

On page 38 John Piper says:

> Since September 11, 2001, I have seen more clearly than ever how essential it is to exult explicitly in the excellence of Christ crucified for sinners and risen from the dead. Christ must be explicit in all our God-talk. It will not do, in this day of pluralism, to talk about the glory of God in vague ways. God without Christ is no God. And a no-God cannot save or satisfy the soul. Following a no-God—whatever his name or whatever his religion—will be a wasted life. God-in-Christ is the only true God and the only path to joy. Everything I have said so far must now be related to Christ. The old kitchen plaque comes back: "Only what's done for Christ will last."

QUESTION 10: When you talk about "God," is it explicit which "god" you are talking about? Do you agree with John Piper's statements above? What Scripture verses could be used to demonstrate these assertions?

DAY 5—REVIEW AND APPLICATION

Review your answers from the previous four days and any parts of *Don't Waste Your Life* that you want and then answer the following questions.

+ **QUESTION 11:** What was the most meaningful part of this chapter for you? Was there a sentence, concept, or idea that really struck you? Record it in the space below.

On page 32 John Piper says the following:

> We waste our lives when we do not pray and think and dream and plan and work toward magnifying God in all spheres of life. God created us for this: to live our lives in a way that makes him look more like the greatness and the beauty and the infinite worth that he really is. In the night sky of this world God appears to most people, if at all, like a pinprick of light in a heaven of darkness. But he created us and called us to make him look like what he really is.

QUESTION 12: When was the last time that you prayed and thought and dreamt and planned and worked toward magnifying God in your life? Write some of the ways that you have endeavored to magnify God and make him look like he really is.

FURTHER UP AND FURTHER IN

On page 23 John Piper says:

> The great Point and Purpose and Essence that I longed to link up with was now connected unbreakably with the Bible. The mandate was clear: "Do your best to present yourself to God as one approved, a worker who has no need to be ashamed, *rightly handling the word of truth*" (2 Timothy 2:15).

He then laments the fact that in academic books and in small groups, Bible study has turned into "a swamp of subjectivity" (page 23).

QUESTION 13: Discuss the relationship between the following two questions as they relate to the study of Scripture. Is one question more important than the other? Should one question be asked before the other? How could misunderstanding the relationship between these two questions keep us from "rightly handling the word of truth"?

A) What did this verse mean to its original audience?

B) What does this verse mean for us today?

QUESTION 14: What is the most beautiful and glorious thing that you have ever seen in nature? Describe the emotions you had when you were beholding such greatness. Were the feelings pleasant or unpleasant?

Now read the following verse from the Psalms.

PSALM 19:1

The heavens declare the glory of God, and the sky above proclaims his handiwork.

What are the heavens declaring? How does this help explain your feelings when you behold great and glorious things in nature?

Many Christians point to John 3:16 in order to show the greatness of God's love for us.

JOHN 3:16

For God so loved the world, that he gave his only Son, that whoever believes in him should not perish but have eternal life.

According to this verse, God loves us by giving us eternal life because we believe in his Son. This strikes most of us as a very loving act on God's part. But what does it mean to "have eternal life"? Look at Jesus' words from his prayer.

JOHN 17:1-5

> [1] *When Jesus had spoken these words, he lifted up his eyes to heaven, and said, "Father, the hour has come; glorify your Son that the Son may glorify you,* [2] *since you have given him authority over all flesh, to give eternal life to all whom you have given him.* [3] *And this is eternal life, that they know you the only true God, and Jesus Christ whom you have sent.* [4] *I glorified you on earth, having accomplished the work that you gave me to do.* [5] *And now, Father, glorify me in your own presence with the glory that I had with you before the world existed."*

QUESTION 15: What is eternal life according to these verses? How does this connection between eternal life and knowing the only true God and Jesus Christ, whom he sent, relate to what you learned in this chapter?

GROUP ACTIVITY

Complete this section during the group time each week.

Break into small groups and spend a few minutes in prayer. In particular, pray that God would awaken in each person a desire to glorify him by being satisfied in all that he is for us in Jesus.

GETTING PRACTICAL

A suggested activity to do in the future: Seek an opportunity to engage with a worldview and perspective that is different from your own. Visit a local mosque, temple, or club, and try to understand how the people who go there view life. Perhaps you would want to make a list of questions about God, Life, Death, Meaning, and Jesus before you go. Ask these questions while you are there. Consider taking friends and family along so they can learn from the experience as well.

NOTES

1. Quoted by John Piper in *Desiring God*, page 19.
2. Quoted by John Piper in *Don't Waste Your Life*, page 29.
3. Excerpt taken from *Desiring God*, page 159.

LESSON 4

BOASTING ONLY IN THE CROSS, THE BLAZING CENTER OF THE GLORY OF GOD

A Companion Study to Don't Waste Your Life, Chapter 3

LESSON OBJECTIVES

It is our prayer that after you have finished this lesson . . .

- You would begin to understand the centrality of the cross for the unwasted life.
- You would discover how the cross can be and *must* be our only boast as Christians.
- The cross would become for you the blazing center of the glory of God.

DAY 1—INITIAL QUESTIONS BEFORE YOU READ

At the end of Chapter 2 John Piper made the following statement:

> Life is wasted if we do not grasp the glory of the cross, cherish it for the treasure that it is, and cleave to it as the highest price of every pleasure and the deepest comfort in every pain. (page 40)

This chapter will explore and explain this statement in more detail.

Read the following passage.

1 CORINTHIANS 2:1-2

[1] *And I, when I came to you, brothers, did not come proclaiming to you the testimony of God with lofty speech or wisdom.*
[2] *For I decided to know nothing among you except Jesus Christ and him crucified.*

QUESTION 1: It is evident from the rest of his letters that Paul was knowledgeable about a great many things (for example, the resurrection and the Holy Spirit and the return of Jesus to earth). How then can he say that he *only* knows "Jesus Christ and him crucified"?

+ QUESTION 2: Make a list of personal attributes that you believe are necessary in order to make a lasting difference in the world. Rank these attributes from the most important to the least important. Which ones do you possess? How can you acquire the ones you don't possess?

DAY 2—IDENTIFYING THE TRUE TRAGEDY

Read from page 43 to the bottom of page 48 in *Don't Waste Your Life* and answer the following questions.

QUESTION 3: According to John Piper, what is necessary to make a lasting difference in the world?

A) A high IQ
B) Great wealth
C) To master a great many things
D) To be mastered by a few things that are very great

On page 45 John Piper says the following:

> You may not be sure that you want your life to make a difference. Maybe you don't care very much whether you make a lasting difference for the sake of something great. You just want people to like you. If people would just like being around you, you'd be satisfied. Or if you could just have a good job with a good wife, or husband, and a couple of good kids and a nice car and long weekends and a few good friends, a fun retirement, and a quick and easy death, and no hell—if you could have all that (even without God)—you would be satisfied. That is a tragedy in the making. A wasted life.

QUESTION 4: Which parts of this description strike you as a tragedy? Do you agree with John Piper that this is a wasted life? Why or why not?

Study the following passage.

PHILIPPIANS 3:7-8

[7] *But whatever gain I had, I counted as loss for the sake of Christ.* [8] *Indeed, I count everything as loss because of the surpassing worth of knowing Christ Jesus my Lord. For his sake I have suffered the loss of all things and count them as rubbish, in order that I may gain Christ.*

+ **QUESTION 5:** According to these verses, what is the apostle Paul's all-embracing passion in life? Restate the main point of these verses in your own words.

DAY 3—THE SHOCKING TRUTH IN GALATIANS 6:14

Read from the bottom of page 48 to the middle of page 54 in *Don't Waste Your Life* and answer the following questions.

Read the following passage.

GALATIANS 6:14

But far be it from me to boast except in the cross of our Lord Jesus Christ, by which the world has been crucified to me, and I to the world.

QUESTION 6: John Piper rephrases this verse positively to say, "Boast only in the cross of our Lord Jesus Christ." Given that in Western culture the cross is a very prominent symbol that people wear as jewelry or put on the back of their car, why is boasting only in the cross so shocking?

Study Romans 5:2-4, 2 Corinthians 12:9, and 1 Thessalonians 2:19-20.

ROMANS 5:2-4

> [2] *Through him we have also obtained access by faith into this grace in which we stand, and we rejoice in hope of the glory of God.* [3] *More than that, we rejoice in our sufferings, knowing that suffering produces endurance,* [4] *and endurance produces character, and character produces hope.*

2 CORINTHIANS 12:9

> *But he said to me, "My grace is sufficient for you, for my power is made perfect in weakness." Therefore I will boast all the more gladly of my weaknesses, so that the power of Christ may rest upon me.*

1 THESSALONIANS 2:19-20

> [19] *For what is our hope or joy or crown of boasting before our Lord Jesus at his coming? Is it not you?* [20] *For you are our glory and joy.*

✦ **QUESTION 7:** In all of these verses Paul speaks of how he boasts in various things.[1] How do we reconcile Galatians 6:14 with these verses that clearly show that Paul himself boasted in, rejoiced in, and exulted in other things besides the cross?

On page 51 John Piper says the following:

> One of the reasons we are not as Christ-centered and cross-centered as we should be is that we have not realized that everything—everything good, and everything bad that God turns for the good of his redeemed children—was purchased by the death of Christ for us. We simply take life and breath and health and friends for granted. We think it is ours by right. But the fact is that it is not ours by right.

QUESTION 8: Do you view life and breath and health and friends through the lens of the cross? Do you take these things for granted and view them as yours by right? What biblical truths have you neglected that lead you to regard these blessings as rights? Cite Scripture verses in your answer.

DAY 4—THE PARADOX OF DYING AND LIVING WITH CHRIST

Read from the middle of page 54 through page 59 in *Don't Waste Your Life* and answer the following questions.

QUESTION 9: Reflect again on Galatians 6:14. Where does boasting only in the cross happen? What does this mean practically? Can you think of other biblical texts that teach this truth?

Study the following passage.

GALATIANS 2:20

I have been crucified with Christ. It is no longer I who live, but Christ who lives in me. And the life I now live in the flesh I live by faith in the Son of God, who loved me and gave himself for me.

✦ **QUESTION 10:** How does it make sense to say that "I" died and yet "I" live? What key words can you find in these verses that explain the difference between the "I" who died and the "I" who lives?

DAY 5—REVIEW AND APPLICATION

Review your answers from the previous four days and any parts of *Don't Waste Your Life* that you want and then answer the following questions.

✦ **QUESTION 11:** What was the most meaningful part of this chapter for you? Was there a sentence, concept, or idea that really struck you? Why? Record your thoughts in the space below.

+ **QUESTION 12:** List four practical steps you can take to make all of your enjoyment in life a "boasting in the cross." (Hint: relate the truth of this chapter to your job or school, your family, your hobbies, and your ministry.)

FURTHER UP AND FURTHER IN

QUESTION 13: Look again at Philippians 3:7-8. What things in your life do you not consider rubbish compared to knowing Jesus Christ? In other words, what do you not count as loss for the sake of gaining Christ?

Study Romans 3:21-26, especially verse 25.

ROMANS 3:21-26

21 But now the righteousness of God has been manifested apart
from the law, although the Law and the Prophets bear witness
to it— 22 the righteousness of God through faith in Jesus Christ
for all who believe. For there is no distinction: 23 for all have
sinned and fall short of the glory of God, 24 and are justified
by his grace as a gift, through the redemption that is in Christ
Jesus, 25 whom God put forward as a propitiation by his blood,
to be received by faith. This was to show God's righteousness,
because in his divine forbearance he had passed over former

> *sins.* [26] *It was to show his righteousness at the present time, so that he might be just and the justifier of the one who has faith in Jesus.*

QUESTION 14: According to these verses, is the cross mainly about our salvation or about the demonstration of God's righteousness? Why did God's righteousness need to be demonstrated?

On pages 49-50 John Piper says the following:

> [Galatians 6:14 is shocking because] it's like saying: Boast only in the electric chair. Only exult in the gas chamber. Only rejoice in the lethal injection. Let your one boast and one joy and one exultation be the lynching rope.

QUESTION 15: If someone said to you, "All of my rejoicing in life can be traced back to the electric chair," or "All of my joy in life can be traced back to the gas chamber," what would be your reaction? Does this help explain why "the word of the cross is folly to those who are perishing" (1 Corinthians 1:18)?

To take up a cross and follow Jesus means to join Jesus on the Calvary Road with a resolve to suffer and die with him. The cross is not a burden to bear; it is an instrument of pain and execution. It would be like saying, "Pick up your electric chair and follow me to the execution room." Or "Pick up this sword and carry it to the place of beheading." Or "Take up this rope and carry it to the gallows."

The domestication of cross-bearing into coughs and cranky spouses takes the radical thrust out of Christ's call. He is calling every believer to "renounce all that he has," to "hate his own life" (Luke 14:33, 26), and to take the road of obedience joyfully, no matter the loss on this earth. Following Jesus means that wherever obedience requires it, we will accept betrayal and rejection and beating and mockery and crucifixion and death. Jesus gives us the assurance that if we will follow him to Golgotha during all the Good Fridays of this life, we will also rise with him on the last Easter day of the resurrection. "Whoever loses his life for my sake and the gospel's will save it" (Mark 8:35). "Whoever hates his life in this world will keep it for eternal life" (John 12:25).[2]

GROUP ACTIVITY

Complete this section during the group time each week.

If we are to understand the centrality of the cross for the unwasted life, we must understand what was accomplished by God through the cross of Jesus Christ. Read the following passages aloud in the group. Briefly discuss how each passage contributes to our understanding of what God achieved for us on the cross. Spend some time praying and thanking God for the sacrifice of his Son, using these texts in your prayers.

GALATIANS 3:13

Christ redeemed us from the curse of the law by becoming a curse for us—for it is written, "Cursed is everyone who is hanged on a tree."

1 PETER 3:18

For Christ also suffered once for sins, the righteous for the unrighteous, that he might bring us to God, being put to death in the flesh but made alive in the spirit.

COLOSSIANS 2:13-15

13 *And you, who were dead in your trespasses and the uncircum-*
cision of your flesh, God made alive together with him, having
forgiven us all our trespasses, 14 *by canceling the record of debt*
that stood against us with its legal demands. This he set aside,
nailing it to the cross. 15 *He disarmed the rulers and authorities*
and put them to open shame, by triumphing over them in him.

2 CORINTHIANS 5:21

For our sake he made him to be sin who knew no sin, so that in him we might become the righteousness of God.

GALATIANS 1:3-4

3 *Grace to you and peace from God our Father and the Lord*
Jesus Christ, 4 *who gave himself for our sins to deliver us from*
the present evil age, according to the will of our God and
Father.

REVELATION 5:9-10

9 *And they sang a new song, saying, "Worthy are you to take*
the scroll and to open its seals, for you were slain, and by your
blood you ransomed people for God from every tribe and
language and people and nation, 10 *and you have made them*
a kingdom and priests to our God, and they shall reign on the
earth."

ROMANS 5:6-10

[6] *For while we were still weak, at the right time Christ died for the ungodly.* [7] *For one will scarcely die for a righteous person—though perhaps for a good person one would dare even to die—* [8] *but God shows his love for us in that while we were still sinners, Christ died for us.* [9] *Since, therefore, we have now been justified by his blood, much more shall we be saved by him from the wrath of God.* [10] *For if while we were enemies we were reconciled to God by the death of his Son, much more, now that we are reconciled, shall we be saved by his life.*

GETTING PRACTICAL

A suggested activity to do in the future: Do a prayer walk around your neighborhood. Pray that God would magnify the worth of his Son through the cross in your neighborhood. Pray that he would show you practical ways that you can minister to your neighbors so that they might come to "boast only in the cross." Perhaps pray through some of the Scriptures in the group activity above. If you have a family, be sure to take them with you and allow them to participate in the joy of seeking God through prayer.

NOTES

1. The Greek word translated "rejoice in" in Romans 5:2-4 is the same word that is translated "boast" in Galatians 6:14 and the other passages.
2. Excerpt taken from *Let the Nations Be Glad*, page 74.

LESSON 5

MAGNIFYING CHRIST THROUGH PAIN AND DEATH

A Companion Study to Don't Waste Your Life, Chapter 4

LESSON OBJECTIVES

It is our prayer that after you have finished this lesson . . .

- You will understand how to honor Christ in life and death.
- You will see the divine design in pain and suffering.
- Philippians 1:21 ("For to me, to live is Christ and to die is gain") will land on you in a powerful and profound way.

DAY 1—INITIAL QUESTIONS BEFORE YOU READ

Study the following passage.

PHILIPPIANS 1:19-26

> 19 *For I know that through your prayers and the help of the*
> *Spirit of Jesus Christ this will turn out for my deliverance,*
> 20 *as it is my eager expectation and hope that I will not be at*
> *all ashamed, but that with full courage now as always Christ*
> *will be honored in my body, whether by life or by death.*

> [21] *For to me to live is Christ, and to die is gain.* [22] *If I am to*
> *live in the flesh, that means fruitful labor for me. Yet which I*
> *shall choose I cannot tell.* [23] *I am hard pressed between the two.*
> *My desire is to depart and be with Christ, for that is far better.*
> [24] *But to remain in the flesh is more necessary on your account.*
> [25] *Convinced of this, I know that I will remain and continue*
> *with you all, for your progress and joy in the faith,* [26] *so that in*
> *me you may have ample cause to glory in Christ Jesus, because*
> *of my coming to you again.*

+ **QUESTION 1:** According to verse 20, what is Paul's eager expectation and hope? How does verse 21 explain this hope? In your own words, restate Paul's main point in verses 19-24.

QUESTION 2: Is there a divine design in our suffering? Does God have purposes for the suffering and pain in your life? If so, what are these purposes? Use the Bible to support your answer.

DAY 2—SHAME, HONOR, AND CHRIST

Read from page 61 to the bottom of page 65 in *Don't Waste Your Life* and answer the following questions.

Look again at Philippians 1:19-26, especially verses 19-20.

QUESTION 3: Normally, shame is the feeling of guilt and failure we experience when we don't measure up. The opposite of being shamed is being honored. What is unusual about Paul's conception of shame and honor?

On page 65 John Piper says the following:

> What you love determines what you feel shame about. If you love for men to make much of you, you will feel shame when they don't. But if you love for men to make much of Christ, then you will feel shame when he is belittled on your account.

+ QUESTION 4: Reflect on times when you have felt ashamed of something you did. Why did you feel that way? What was it that you loved that ultimately led to shame?

DAY 3—HONORING CHRIST IN LIFE AND DEATH

Read from the bottom of page 65 to the top of page 71 in *Don't Waste Your Life* and answer the following questions.

+ **QUESTION 5:** Turn back to Lesson 2 in this study guide and review your answers to Question 1. Does death threaten these goals? Does death threaten your ultimate goal in life? Why or why not?

> Death is a threat to the degree that it frustrates your main goals. Death is fearful to the degree that it threatens to rob you of what you treasure most. But Paul treasured Christ most, and his goal was to magnify Christ. And he saw death not as the frustration of that goal but as an occasion for its fulfillment. (page 66)

+ **QUESTION 6:** Based on Philippians 1:19-26 and your reading of this section in *Don't Waste Your Life*, explain the following statements in your own words:

A) "To live is Christ."

B) "To die is gain."

QUESTION 7: Explain the following sentence: "The essence of praising Christ is prizing Christ" (page 68). Use Scripture in your answer.

DAY 4—DIVINE DESIGN IN OUR AFFLICTIONS

Read from the top of page 71 through page 76 in *Don't Waste Your Life* and answer the following questions.

Study the following passage.

2 CORINTHIANS 1:8-9

> [8] *For we do not want you to be ignorant, brothers, of the afflic-*
> *tion we experienced in Asia. For we were so utterly burdened*
> *beyond our strength that we despaired of life itself.* [9] *Indeed, we*
> *felt that we had received the sentence of death. But that was to*
> *make us rely not on ourselves but on God who raises the dead.*

QUESTION 8: According to these verses, what was the divine design in Paul's experience of affliction? In light of this design, is it right to say that God sent the affliction into Paul's life? Can you think of other biblical examples to support your argument?

✦ **QUESTION 9:** Which is more impressive:

A) To get rich and thank God

or

B) to be so satisfied in God that you give away riches and call it gain?

Why did you choose the answer that you did?

QUESTION 10: Does the call to suffer pain and even death for the cause of Christ mean that Christians are suicidal? Is there a legitimate place for enjoying God's gifts?

DAY 5—REVIEW AND APPLICATION

Review your answers from the previous four days and any parts of *Don't Waste Your Life* that you want and then answer the following questions.

+ **QUESTION 11:** What was the most meaningful part of this chapter for you? Was there a sentence, concept, or idea that really struck you? Why? Record your thoughts in the space below.

QUESTION 12: In this chapter Piper argues that "Death makes visible where our treasure is" (page 68) and "Christ aims to be magnified in life most clearly by the way we experience him in our losses" (page 73). Think about the last time you experienced a significant loss. What did your response to this loss indicate about where your treasure is? Record your reflections below.

FURTHER UP AND FURTHER IN

Study the following passage.

HEBREWS 13:12-14

> [12] *So Jesus also suffered outside the gate in order to sanctify the*
> *people through his own blood.* [13] *Therefore let us go to him*
> *outside the camp and bear the reproach he endured.* [14] *For here*
> *we have no lasting city, but we seek the city that is to come.*

QUESTION 13: In a sermon delivered at Wheaton College, John Piper said, in regard to the passage above, "Golgotha is not a suburb of Jerusalem."[1] What do you think he meant by that statement? In your own words, describe what it means to "go to him outside the camp." According to these verses, where does the strength to bear the reproach of Jesus come from? (Hint: notice the word "For" in verse 14.)

> We measure the worth of a hidden treasure by what we will gladly sell to buy it. If we will sell all, then we measure the worth as supreme. If we will not, what we have is treasured more. "The kingdom of heaven is like a treasure hidden in a field, which a man found and covered up. Then *in his joy* he goes and sells *all that he has* and buys that field" (Matt. 13:44). The extent of his *sacrifice* and the depth of his *joy* display the worth he puts on the treasure of God. Loss and suffering, joyfully accepted for the kingdom of God, show the supremacy of God's worth more clearly in the world than all worship and prayer.[2]

QUESTION 14: In light of what you've learned in this chapter, do you agree with the last sentence in the above quotation? How is it that our losses and sufferings, when they are joyfully accepted for the kingdom of God, show God's worth more than all worship and prayer? Can you find other places in Scripture where this is demonstrated?

Study 1 Corinthians 15:19 and the quote from John Piper that follows.

1 CORINTHIANS 15:19

If in this life only we have hoped in Christ, we are of all people most to be pitied.

> It seems that most Christians in the prosperous West describe the benefits of Christianity in terms that would make it a good

> life, even if there were no God and no resurrection. Think of all the psychological benefits and relational benefits. And of course these are true and biblical: The fruit of the Holy Spirit is love, joy, and peace. So if we get love, joy, and peace from believing these things, then is it not a good life to live, even if it turns out to be based on a falsehood? Why should we be pitied?
>
> What's wrong with Paul, then? Was he not living the abundant life? Why would he say that if there is no resurrection, we are of all men most to be pitied? . . .
>
> The answer seems to be that the Christian life for Paul was not the so-called good life of prosperity and ease. Instead it was a life of freely chosen suffering beyond anything we normally experience.[3]

QUESTION 15: In light of the above statements, can you say the following about your life: "The lifestyle I have chosen as a Christian would be utterly foolish and pitiable if there is no resurrection"? Or again, can you say, "The suffering I have freely chosen to embrace for Christ would be a pitiable life if there is no resurrection"?[4] Explain your answer.

GROUP ACTIVITY

Complete this section during the group time each week.

Instruct one person to read the following story aloud to the group. Then discuss how this story connects to the material from this week's lesson.

One of the unlikeliest men to attend the Itinerant Evangelists' Conference in Amsterdam sponsored by the Billy Graham Association was a Masai Warrior named Joseph. But his story won him a hearing with Dr. Graham himself. The story is told by Michael Card.

> One day, Joseph, who was walking along one of these hot, dirty African roads, met someone who shared the gospel of Jesus Christ with him. Then and there he accepted Jesus as his Lord and Savior. The power of the Spirit began transforming his life; he was filled with such excitement and joy that the first thing he wanted to do was return to his own village and share the same Good News with the members of his local tribe.
>
> Joseph began going from door-to-door, telling everyone he met about the Cross of Jesus and the salvation it offered, expecting to see their faces light up the way his had. To his amazement the villagers not only didn't care, they became violent. The men of the village seized him and held him to the ground while the women beat him with strands of barbed wire. He was dragged from the village and left to die alone in the bush.
>
> Joseph somehow managed to crawl to a waterhole, and there, after days of passing in and out of consciousness, found the strength to get up. He wondered about the hostile reception he had received from people he had known all his life. He decided he must have left something out or told the story of Jesus incorrectly. After rehearsing the message he had first heard, he decided to go back and share his faith once more.
>
> Joseph limped into the circle of huts and began to proclaim Jesus. "He died for you, so that you might find forgiveness and come to know the living God," he pleaded. Again he was grabbed by the men of the village and held while the women beat him, reopening wounds that had just begun to heal. Once more they dragged him unconscious from the village and left him to die.

> To have survived the first beating was truly remarkable. To live through the second was a miracle. Again, days later, Joseph awoke in the wilderness, bruised, scarred—and determined to go back.
>
> He returned to the small village and this time, they attacked him before he had a chance to open his mouth. As they flogged him for the third and probably the last time, he again spoke to them of Jesus Christ, the Lord. Before he passed out, the last thing he saw was that the women who were beating him began to weep.
>
> This time he awoke in his own bed. The ones who had so severely beaten him were now trying to save his life and nurse him back to health. The entire village had come to Christ.[5]

GETTING PRACTICAL

A suggested activity to do in the future: Seek an opportunity to minister to someone who is sick or enduring suffering. Consult with your pastor, and offer to visit the sick in a hospital or nursing home. Try to encourage them with Scripture and by praying with them. If you have a family, take them with you so they too can share in the joy of ministering to the sick and suffering.

NOTES

1. Quote taken from "Doing Missions When Dying Is Gain," a sermon included on Desiring God's "Light and Heat" Audio CD.
2. Excerpt taken from *Let the Nations Be Glad*, page 71.
3. Excerpt taken from *Desiring God*, page 255.
4. Questions taken from *Desiring God*, page 261.
5. Excerpt taken from *Let the Nations Be Glad*, pages 93-94.

LESSON 6

RISK IS RIGHT—BETTER TO LOSE YOUR LIFE THAN TO WASTE IT *AND* THE GOAL OF LIFE—GLADLY MAKING OTHERS GLAD IN GOD

A Companion Study to Don't Waste Your Life, Chapters 5 and 6

LESSON OBJECTIVES

It is our prayer that after you have finished this lesson . . .

- The myth of safety around your life will have been exploded by the Bible.
- You will be propelled by the promises of God to embrace more risk for the cause of Christ.
- You will make it your ambition in life to gladly make others glad in God.

DAY 1—INITIAL QUESTIONS BEFORE YOU READ

In these chapters we will explore the role of risk in the Christian life and see how faith in the promises of God compels us to lay down our lives to make others glad in God.

QUESTION 1: Give a short definition of *risk*. Do you naturally move toward or away from risk? Give three ways that you seek to insulate yourself from risk.

+ **QUESTION 2:** Is there a distinction between good risk and bad risk? If so, what is the difference? Provide two examples of good risk and two examples of bad risk. Be sure to explain what makes them examples of good or bad risk.

QUESTION 3: Is "gladly making others glad in God" identical to loving others? If that is to be our goal in life, how does it relate to other goals in life that we have discussed in previous lessons like "Boast only in the cross" and "Pursue the glory of God"?

DAY 2—EXPLODING MYTHS AND TAKING RISKS

Read from page 79 to the middle of page 89 in *Don't Waste Your Life* and answer the following questions.

Study the following passage.

JAMES 4:13-15

[13] *Come now, you who say, "Today or tomorrow we will go into such and such a town and spend a year there and trade and make a profit"—* [14] *yet you do not know what tomorrow will bring. What is your life? For you are a mist that appears for a little time and then vanishes.* [15] *Instead you ought to say, "If the Lord wills, we will live and do this or that."*

On page 81 John Piper says the following:

> Therefore risk is woven into the fabric of our finite lives. We cannot avoid risk even if we want to. Ignorance and uncertainty about tomorrow is our native air. All of our plans for tomorrow's activities can be shattered by a thousand unknowns whether we stay at home under the covers or ride the freeways. One of my aims is to explode the myth of safety and to somehow deliver you from the enchantment of security. Because it's a mirage. It doesn't exist. Every direction you turn there are unknowns and things beyond your control.

QUESTION 4: In light of this, should we stop putting locks on our doors? Is John Piper advocating that we take risks merely for the sake of risk? Explain your answer.

QUESTION 5: From page 81 to page 87 John Piper gives numerous biblical examples of people who risked. He cites Joab;

Esther; Shadrach, Meshach, and Abednego; Paul; and Jesus. Choose one of these examples and meditate on it. How was risk present in his or her or their situation? What was the God-honoring response of the person(s) in the story to the risk that was present? Record your reflections below.

DAY 3: MORE THAN CONQUERORS

Read from the middle of page 89 through page 98 in *Don't Waste Your Life* and answer the following questions.

QUESTION 6: On page 90 John Piper says there are good reasons to risk and bad reasons to risk. What is the difference between the good reasons and the bad reasons? How does Piper's idea of risk differ from thrill-seekers who jump out of airplanes or off cliffs?

Study the following words of Jesus.

LUKE 21:16-19

16 *You will be delivered up even by parents and brothers and relatives and friends, and some of you they will put to death.*

[17] You will be hated by all for my name's sake. [18] But not a hair of your head will perish. [19] By your endurance you will gain your lives.

+ **QUESTION 7:** Explain these verses in your own words. "Some of you they will put to death. . . . But not a hair of your head will perish." How can both of these statements be true?

Study the following passage.

ROMANS 8:35-39

[35] Who shall separate us from the love of Christ? Shall tribulation, or distress, or persecution, or famine, or nakedness, or danger, or sword? [36] As it is written, "For your sake we are being killed all the day long; we are regarded as sheep to be slaughtered." [37] No, in all these things we are more than conquerors through him who loved us. [38] For I am sure that neither death nor life, nor angels nor rulers, nor things present nor things to come, nor powers, [39] nor height nor depth, nor anything else in all creation, will be able to separate us from the love of God in Christ Jesus our Lord.

+ **QUESTION 8:** What does it mean to be a conqueror? What does it mean to be more than a conqueror? Apply this distinction to the following verse from Ephesians 6. What would it mean to conquer "the flaming darts of the evil one"? What would it mean to more-than-conquer them?

EPHESIANS 6:16

[16] *In all circumstances take up the shield of faith, with which you can extinguish all the flaming darts of the evil one.*

DAY 4—PURSUING OUR JOY IN THE JOY OF OTHERS

Read from page 99 through page 105 in *Don't Waste Your Life* and answer the following questions.

QUESTION 9: Why shouldn't any of the following reasons be the *ultimate* reason for wanting forgiveness?

- To be cleansed from a guilty conscience
- To escape the pain of hell
- To go to heaven to see our loved ones

What makes these gifts ultimately good?

Study 2 Corinthians 1:24 and Galatians 5:22-23.

2 CORINTHIANS 1:24

Not that we lord it over your faith, but we work with you for your joy, for you stand firm in your faith.

GALATIANS 5:22-23

> [22] *But the fruit of the Spirit is love, joy, peace, patience, kindness, goodness, faithfulness,* [23] *gentleness, self-control; against such things there is no law.*

✦ **QUESTION 10:** How can Paul say that he works with them for their joy and that joy is a fruit of the Spirit? Who produces joy in people—us or God? Can you think of other verses that describe this tension?

DAY 5—REVIEW AND APPLICATION

Review your answers from the previous four days and any parts of *Don't Waste Your Life* that you want and then answer the following questions.

✦ **QUESTION 11:** What was the most meaningful part of these chapters for you? Was there a sentence, concept, or idea that really struck you? Why? Record your thoughts in the space below.

+ **QUESTION 12:** Make a list of six practical ways that a person could risk more for the cause of Christ. Circle the ones that you can immediately apply to your situation.

FURTHER UP AND FURTHER IN

QUESTION 13: John Piper defines a risk as "an action that exposes you to the possibility of loss or injury" (page 79). He also notes that the reason risk exists is "because there is such a thing as ignorance" (page 80). In light of this definition, is it possible for God to take risks? Has God ever taken a risk? Use Scripture to support your answer.

Study the following passage.

MATTHEW 6:25, 31-33

25 Therefore I tell you, do not be anxious about your life, what
you will eat or what you will drink, nor about your body, what
you will put on. Is not life more than food, and the body more
than clothing? . . . 31 Therefore do not be anxious, saying,
"What shall we eat?" or "What shall we drink?" or "What shall
we wear?" 32 For the Gentiles seek after all these things, and

your heavenly Father knows that you need them all. [33] *But seek first the kingdom of God and his righteousness, and all these things will be added to you.*

QUESTION 14: How do we reconcile these verses that promise that God will supply our basic needs with the obvious reality that some Christians die of hunger and thirst and exposure? Are there other Scriptures that speak to this issue?

On page 97 John Piper says, "Faith in these promises frees us to risk and to find in our own experience that it is better to lose our life than to waste it." If the power to risk comes from the promises of God, then it is necessary for us to lay hold of God's promises in Scripture so that we embrace risk for the sake of Christ. Study the following promise in Romans, and answer the question below.

ROMANS 8:31-32

[31] *What then shall we say to these things? If God is for us, who can be against us?* [32] *He who did not spare his own Son but gave him up for us all, how will he not also with him graciously give us all things?*

QUESTION 15: It is obvious that many things can be against us. Satan, sin, the world, other people—all of these (and more!) can be against us. What, then, does verse 31 mean? How does it work as a promise? How does the logic of verse 32 work?

GROUP ACTIVITY

Complete this section during the group time each week.

Discuss the following hypothetical examples in your small group. Are these examples of acceptable risk? In other words, is risk "right" in these examples? Give reasons for your decision.

A) A missionary takes his wife and three children to a country in Africa where there has been ongoing warfare between rival tribes. As a result of the warfare, two other missionaries have been killed within the past year.

B) A college student spends his summer traveling illegally to and from a country where spreading Christianity is against the law, taking Bibles in the native language and distributing them to the people.

C) A missionary team in Central Asia find themselves embroiled in a dispute with local religious leaders in their area. An armed mob with machetes surrounds their compound, threatening to kill everyone inside. The mob decides to give the missionaries three weeks to leave the country or else. The mission agency recommends that the team withdraw until the tension subsides. The missionaries ignore the recommendation and decide to stay in the country.

D) A family from the suburbs of a major U.S. city decides to move into an urban ghetto in order to magnify Christ among the poor. Their four children, who each had their own rooms in their former house, are forced to share one room. Their neighborhood is home to crack houses, gangs, and prostitution.

GETTING PRACTICAL

A suggested activity to do in the future: Look for opportunities in your community to meet the practical needs of people. Volunteer at a local food shelter or soup kitchen. Offer to cook a meal for someone who is going through a difficult time. Do yard work for someone who is unable to do it him- or herself. If you're not sure where to look for needs, consult your pastor or church secretary. If you have a family, include them in the experience of loving people in practical and tangible ways.

SPECIAL ASSIGNMENT FOR LESSON 7

Complete the following assignment during the week prior to the group discussion on Lesson 7.

Turn to Appendix C: Weekly Activity Log. Using this log, keep track of the amount of time you spend this week doing each listed activity. Be prepared to discuss this material during the group discussion on Lesson 7.

LESSON 7

LIVING TO PROVE HE IS MORE PRECIOUS THAN LIFE

A Companion Study to Don't Waste Your Life, Chapter 7

LESSON OBJECTIVES

It is our prayer that after you have finished this lesson . . .

- You will endeavor to use your money to demonstrate the worth and value of Jesus Christ.
- You will embrace a strategic wartime lifestyle that aims to magnify Christ in the world.
- You will begin to dream about feats of courage and sacrifice in the service of Christ.

DAY 1—INITIAL QUESTIONS BEFORE YOU READ

+ **QUESTION 1:** If someone who did not know that you were a Christian observed the way you spend your money, the kind of clothes you wear, the way you spend your free time, and how you raised your family, would they notice a significant difference between you and the world? What sort of differences would they notice?

Study the following verses.

MARK 10:21

[Jesus said] You lack one thing: go, sell all you have and give to the poor, and you will have treasure in heaven; and come, follow me.

LUKE 6:20, 24

[20] *Blessed are you who are poor, for yours is the kingdom of God. . . .* [24] *But woe to you who are rich, for you have received your consolation.*

LUKE 18:25

It is easier for a camel to go through the eye of a needle than for a rich person to enter the kingdom of God.

+ QUESTION 2: What is the common theme in these texts? Underline this theme in each verse. What is your understanding of Jesus' words? How are you currently seeking to obey these texts in your life? Be specific.

Study the following passage.

EPHESIANS 5:15-17

[15] *Look carefully then how you walk, not as unwise but as wise,*
[16] *making the best use of the time, because the days are evil.*
[17] *Therefore do not be foolish, but understand what the will of the Lord is.*

QUESTION 3: What is the main point of this passage? List three ways that you "make the best use of the time." List three ways that you fail to "make the best use of the time." What consequences do you see in your life from wasting your time in these ways?

DAY 2—LIFE IS WAR

Read from page 107 to the bottom of page 114 in *Don't Waste Your Life* and answer the following questions.

QUESTION 4: On page 109 John Piper notes that "The issue of money and lifestyle is not a side issue in the Bible. The credibility of Christ in the world hangs on it." Slowly review the texts dealing with money on pages 109-110. Summarize the teaching of these verses in your own words. Which text is the most meaningful to you at this point in your life? Why?

QUESTION 5: Review Ralph Winter's description of the *Queen Mary* in peacetime and wartime (pages 112-113). Does your life look more like the *Queen Mary* in peacetime or wartime?

Give reasons for your choice. Can you think of any luxuries that you call "needs"? If so, list them.

✦ **QUESTION 6:** Define wartime lifestyle. How does it differ from a simple lifestyle? Does a wartime lifestyle mean that we never seek to raise large amounts of money? What Bible verses might support the idea of a wartime lifestyle?

> In wartime, the newspapers carry headlines about how the troops are doing. In wartime, families talk about the sons and daughters on the front lines and write to them and pray for them with heart-wrenching concern for their safety. In wartime, we are on the alert. We are armed. We are vigilant. In wartime, we spend money differently—there is austerity, not for its own sake but because there are more strategic ways to spend money than on new tires at home. The war effort touches everybody. We all cut back. The luxury liner becomes a troop carrier.[1]

DAY 3—AVOIDING SIN AND WASTING LIFE

Read from page 115 to the middle of page 122 in *Don't Waste Your Life* and answer the following questions.

QUESTION 7: On pages 118-119 John Piper notes that the way we approach life (wartime vs. peacetime) and ethics (avoidance vs. treasuring Christ) affects the kinds of questions that we ask about our behavior. Pick two specific behaviors or choices, and examine them in light of the different sets of questions on these pages. Record your observations below.

On page 120 John Piper says the following:

> Television is one of the greatest life-wasters of the modern age. And, of course, the Internet is running to catch up, and may have caught up. . . . The main problem with TV is not how much smut is available, though that is a problem. Just the ads are enough to sow fertile seeds of greed and lust, no matter what program you're watching. The greater problem is banality. A mind fed daily on TV diminishes. Your mind was made to know and love God. Its facility for this great calling is ruined by excessive TV. The content is so trivial and so shallow that the capacity of the mind to think worthy thoughts withers, and the capacity of the heart to feel deep emotions shrivels.

John Piper singles out television and Internet as great life-wasters. No one will ever say on their deathbed, "I wish I had spent more time in front of the TV or surfing the Internet."

QUESTION 8: What is the biggest problem with TV? List three ways that television and the Internet negatively affect you and your family. If someone compared the amount of time you spent watching television and surfing the Internet with the amount of combined time you spent praying, reading the Bible, and worshiping God, what might they conclude about the source of your satisfaction?

DAY 4—CLEARING THE FOG

Read from the middle of page 122 to page 129 in *Don't Waste Your Life* and answer the following questions.

✦ **QUESTION 9:** In this section John Piper discusses the courage and sacrifices of soldiers in World War II. What is the point of dwelling on these stories? What connection does John Piper want us to make to our lives?

QUESTION 10: In this chapter John Piper confronts our modern obsession with trivial things. Make a list of at least six items to which people devote significant amounts of time and money. Then circle the ones to which you personally devote too much time or money. In light of this chapter, what action, if any, are you planning to take with respect to these passions?

DAY 5—REVIEW AND APPLICATION

Review your answers from the previous four days and any parts of *Don't Waste Your Life* that you want and then answer the following questions.

✦ **QUESTION 11:** What was the most meaningful part of this chapter for you? Was there a sentence, concept, or idea that really struck you? Why? Record your thoughts in the space below.

✦ **QUESTION 12:** In this chapter John Piper talked about times when "the trifling fog of life clears and I see what I am really on earth to do" (page 125). Is the fog clearing over your life? What are you seeing clearly? List three changes you believe God is calling you to make. Share them during the small group time.

FURTHER UP AND FURTHER IN

Read the following hypothetical story.

Joe just lost his job as a security guard. He receives his last paycheck. He is not sure how he will be able to pay his living expenses next month. Despite his tough situation, when he goes to church he gives his normal tithe, 10 percent of his paycheck. More than that, he also contributes to the "Special Needs" offering to provide food for orphans in Africa. Later he receives a call from a close friend who doesn't have any medical insurance but needs to see a doctor about heart problems. Joe lends him the money. Before long Joe has given away almost his entire paycheck.

QUESTION 13: Is Joe being a good steward or is he being foolish? What would you do in his situation? How does this story compare to the story of the widow and her last two pennies in Luke 21:1-4.

Study the following passage.

2 CORINTHIANS 8:1-5

1 We want you to know, brothers, about the grace of God that
has been given among the churches of Macedonia, 2 for in a
severe test of affliction, their abundance of joy and their extreme
poverty have overflowed in a wealth of generosity on their part.
3 For they gave according to their means, as I can testify, and
beyond their means, of their own free will, 4 begging us earnestly
for the favor of taking part in the relief of the saints— 5 and this,

not as we expected, but they gave themselves first to the Lord and then by the will of God to us.

QUESTION 14: In this passage, what three factors came together to overflow in a wealth of generosity? Underline the parts of this passage that you judge to be most countercultural in our modern society. According to this passage, is abundant giving a heavy burden or a divine blessing?

My conviction is that one of the main reasons the world and the church are awash in lust and pornography (by both men and women—30 percent of Internet pornography is now viewed by women) is that our lives are intellectually and emotionally disconnected from the infinite, soul-staggering grandeur for which we were made. Inside and outside the church Western culture is drowning in a sea of triviality, pettiness, banality, and silliness. Television is trivial. Radio is trivial. Conversation is trivial. Education is trivial. Christian books are trivial. Worship styles are trivial. It is inevitable that the human heart, which was made to be staggered with the supremacy of Christ, but instead is drowning in a sea of banal entertainment, will reach for the best natural buzz that life can give: sex.[2]

QUESTION 15: Interact with the paragraph above. Do you think it is an accurate assessment of why sexual immorality is so prevalent in Western society and the church? Why or why not? If this is a description of the "disease," what do you think is the cure? Be specific in what you prescribe, and cite Scripture in your answer.

GROUP ACTIVITY

Complete this section during the group time each week.

Break up into groups of three or four. Share the results of your Weekly Activity Log with your group. Discuss the activities that you spent the most time doing. Share one activity that you would like to cut back on in your life. Pray together that God would give each person the grace to avoid spending time on life-wasting activities.

GETTING PRACTICAL

A suggested activity to do in the future: Begin to budget money each month to support a missionary effort. Ask your pastor about missionaries from your church. Perhaps write a missionary family a letter to encourage them in their faith. If you have a family, include them in this activity. Put a picture of the missionary or missionary family near your kitchen table, and pray for him or her or them during a meal.

NOTES

1. Excerpt taken from *Let the Nations Be Glad*, pages 47-48.
2. Excerpt taken from *Sex and the Supremacy of Christ*, page 44.

LESSON 8

MAKING MUCH OF CHRIST FROM 8 TO 5

A Companion Study to Don't Waste Your Life, Chapter 8

LESSON OBJECTIVES

It is our prayer that after you have finished this lesson . . .

- You will better understand what it means to be made in the image of God.
- Your vocation will take on greater significance as you discover multiple ways to honor God in your work.
- God will have so moved in your heart that you are emboldened to live and preach the Gospel at your workplace.

DAY 1—INITIAL QUESTIONS BEFORE YOU READ

This chapter will explore some fundamental ways to magnify Christ in your daily life. However, the chapter title could be misleading. It might give the impression that only those with full- or part-time jobs need to read this chapter. This conclusion would be a mistake. The truths in this chapter apply not only to those who work in secular vocations but also to high school and college students, homemakers, and those who work from home rather than from an office. If you are in any of these last groups, we urge you to apply the truths of the chapter to whatever "work" (whether office, school, or domestic) God has called you to perform.

QUESTION 1: Many people in the church divide vocations into two types—secular and sacred. In your mind, what is the difference between a secular vocation and a sacred one? Give two examples of each. Is one type of vocation more spiritual than the other? Why or why not? Give Scripture verses that bear on this issue.

Study Colossians 3:23-24 and 1 Corinthians 15:58.

COLOSSIANS 3:23-24

> [23] *Whatever you do, work heartily, as for the Lord and not for men,* [24] *knowing that from the Lord you will receive the inheritance as your reward. You are serving the Lord Christ.*

1 CORINTHIANS 15:58

> *Therefore, my beloved brothers, be steadfast, immovable, always abounding in the work of the Lord, knowing that in the Lord your labor is not in vain.*

+ QUESTION 2: Do these verses *only* apply to Christian ministry? Or do they apply to secular jobs as well? List three practical ways to obey these commands in your vocation.

+ **QUESTION 3:** Both of these passages give an incentive for obedience. What is the incentive in each? (Hint: in both verses it begins with the word "knowing.") How does "knowing" these things function as an incentive to obey the above commands?

DAY 2—GOING TO WORK WITH GOD

Read from page 131 to the middle of page 138 in *Don't Waste Your Life* and answer the following questions.

+ **QUESTION 4:** How would you respond to someone who said, "The only vocations that truly honor God are those that are explicitly Christian, like that of a pastor or a missionary"? Be sure to cite Scripture in your answer.

QUESTION 5: What does it mean to go to work (or school) "with God"? Describe three ways that you currently take God to work (or school) with you.

DAY 3—IMAGE-BEARERS ON THE JOB

Read from the middle of page 138 to the middle of page 144 in *Don't Waste Your Life* and answer the following questions.

On pages 138-139 John Piper says the following:

> Our creation in God's image leads directly to our privilege and duty to *subdue* the earth and *have dominion* over it. In other words, we should be busy understanding and shaping and designing and using God's creation in a way that calls attention to his worth and wakens worship. . . . This implies that part of what it means to be human is to exercise lordship over creation and give the world shape and order and design that reflects the truth and beauty of God.

+ **QUESTION 6:** Consider the following vocations. How does each one "give the world shape and order and design that reflects the truth and beauty of God"?

A) Electrician

B) Third grade teacher

C) Accountant

D) Medical doctor

E) Your vocation

Study the following passage.

TITUS 2:9-10

[9] Slaves are to be submissive to their own masters in everything; they are to be well-pleasing, not argumentative, [10] not pilfering, but showing all good faith, so that in everything they may adorn the doctrine of God our Savior.

On page 143 John Piper says the following about this passage:

> In other words, our work is not the beautiful woman, but the necklace. The beautiful woman is the Gospel—"the doctrine of God our Savior." So one crucial meaning of our secular work is that the way we do it will increase or decrease the attractiveness of the gospel we profess before unbelievers.

QUESTION 7: Make a list of five things that Christians do that decrease the attractiveness of the Gospel. Then make a list of five things that Christians do that increase the attractiveness of the Gospel.

DAY 4—LABORING FOR ETERNAL FOOD

Read from the middle of page 144 to page 154 in *Don't Waste Your Life* and answer the following questions.

Study Genesis 2:15 and 3:17-19.

GENESIS 2:15

The LORD God took the man and put him in the garden of Eden to work it and keep it.

GENESIS 3:17-19

[17] *And to Adam he said, "Because you have listened to the voice of your wife and have eaten of the tree of which I commanded you, 'You shall not eat of it,' cursed is the ground because of you; in pain you shall eat of it all the days of your life;* [18] *thorns and thistles it shall bring forth for you; and you shall eat the plants of the field.* [19] *By the sweat of your face you shall eat bread, till you return to the ground, for out of it you were taken; for you are dust, and to dust you shall return."*

QUESTION 8: According to these verses, is work itself a curse? How do you know? If you said no to the first question, what exactly is the curse? List three ways that you see this curse manifested in your line of work (whether you are in a secular vocation, a homemaker, or a student).

+ QUESTION 9: Should the main goal of our working be to make money? If not, what should be the goal of our labor? Be sure to cite Scripture verses in your answer. List three ways that you can pursue this goal in your workplace.

QUESTION 10: The sixth way to make much of Christ in the workplace that John Piper mentions is personal evangelism. "[God] has woven you into the fabric of others' lives so that you will tell them the Gospel" (page 151). In the space below, describe an instance when you have shared the Gospel with someone in your workplace (or classroom). If you've never done this, think of a few practical ways in which you might initiate an opportunity to share the Gospel in the future.

DAY 5—REVIEW AND APPLICATION

Review your answers from the previous four days and any parts of *Don't Waste Your Life* that you want and then answer the following questions.

+ **QUESTION 11:** What was the most meaningful part of this chapter for you? Was there a sentence, concept, or idea that really struck you? Why? Record your thoughts in the space below.

On page 153 John Piper says the following:

> For many of you the move toward missions and deeds of mercy will not be a move away from your work but with your work to another, more needy, less-reached part of the world. Christians should seriously ask not only what their vocation is, but where it should be lived out. We should not assume that teachers and carpenters and computer programmers and managers and CPAs and doctors and pilots should do their work in America. That very vocation may be better used in a country that is otherwise hard to get into, or in a place where poverty makes access to the Gospel difficult.

+ QUESTION 12: List three reasons why you chose to enter the particular line of work that you are in. Now list three reasons why you chose to do that work in the particular location that you chose. In light of what you've been learning in this book, were these God-honoring reasons to pick this location? Are there any stirrings of desire in you to do your current work in "another, more needy, less-reached part of the world"? Record your thoughts in the space below.

FURTHER UP AND FURTHER IN

QUESTION 13: In this chapter John Piper discussed the principle of "Taking the Promises to Work" (page 137). As you spend time in the Bible over the next few weeks, make a list of verses and passages of Scripture that you could take to work. Perhaps write them on index cards and carry them with you to work.

Study Ephesians 4:28 and 1 Thessalonians 4:11-12.

EPHESIANS 4:28

Let the thief no longer steal, but rather let him labor, doing honest work with his own hands, so that he may have something to share with anyone in need.

1 THESSALONIANS 4:11-12

[11] *. . . aspire to live quietly, and to mind your own affairs, and to work with your hands, as we instructed you,* [12] *so that you may live properly before outsiders and be dependent on no one.*

QUESTION 14: What is the common theme of these two passages? (Hint: look for the common phrase.) In each passage this common theme has a different purpose. What is the purpose given in each passage? Under which of John Piper's six reasons does each purpose belong?

Study the following passage.

2 THESSALONIANS 3:10-12

[10] *For even when we were with you, we would give you this command: If anyone is not willing to work, let him not eat.*
[11] *For we hear that some among you walk in idleness, not busy at work, but busybodies.* [12] *Now such persons we command and encourage in the Lord Jesus Christ to do their work quietly and to earn their own living.*

QUESTION 15: What sin does this passage warn against? What is the consequence of committing this sin in the given passage? What do you think the difference is between being "busy at work" and being "busybodies"? In light of what you've learned in this chapter, why is this sin such a big deal?

GROUP ACTIVITY

Complete this section during the group time each week.

Complete the following activity:

- Divide into two groups.
- Let each group make a list of all the occupations represented in that group.
- Trade lists.
- Think of practical ways to apply the truths in this chapter to the other group's occupations. Try to be as specific as possible.
- Let each group compare its ideas with the other group's, and encourage people to try to implement some of them.

GETTING PRACTICAL

A suggested activity to do in the future: Seek an opportunity to share the Gospel with the unbelieving coworker, friend, or family member you have been praying for since Lesson 2. Perhaps you could begin such a conversation by asking him or her what he or she considers to be a meaningful and significant (unwasted) life.

LESSON 9

THE MAJESTY OF CHRIST IN MISSIONS AND MERCY—A PLEA TO THIS GENERATION

A Companion Study to Don't Waste Your Life, Chapter 9

LESSON OBJECTIVES

It is our prayer that after you have finished this lesson . . .

- You will begin to understand God's global purposes for worship and mission.
- A passion for God's glory among the nations will be awakened in your heart.
- You will prayerfully consider how God might be calling you to express this passion in either going or sending.

DAY 1—INITIAL QUESTIONS BEFORE YOU READ

Before we are able to discuss the majesty of Christ in missions and mercy, it is necessary and helpful to define our terms. It is common in churches to hear someone say, "God calls all Christians to preach the Gospel. Therefore we're all missionaries, no matter where we live or what we do." While this is certainly true in one sense, calling every Christian a missionary can sometimes create confusion about different types of ministries. Therefore, for the purposes of this study we have chosen to distinguish between evangelism and missions. Evangelism is the ministry of a local church to preach the Gospel to people of the same cultural background as those within the church. The aim of evangelism is to win as many people as possible where the church exists. Missions, on the other hand, is an activity of the church that seeks to establish churches among all the various people groups throughout the world. The aim of missions is that "there be a church who worships God through Jesus Christ in all the peoples and tribes and languages and ethnic groups of the world."[1] According to this definition, missions has to be cross-cultural. Under the umbrella of *missions*, missiologists (scholars who study missions) often distinguish between "regular missions" and "frontier missions." Regular missions is "cross-cultural Christian work that spreads the gospel within people groups where churches have already been established." Frontier missions is "cross-cultural Christian work that seeks to establish churches within people groups where it does not yet exist"[2]—in other words, in "unreached people groups," a term that will come up in your reading.

✦ **QUESTION 1:** In the space below, describe your current involvement in world missions. This would include prayer, financial support, mission trips, and current plans for the future.

Study Psalm 67 and Revelation 5:9-12.

PSALM 67

[1] May God be gracious to us and bless us
and make his face to shine upon us,
[2] that your way may be known on earth,
your saving power among all nations.
[3] Let the peoples praise you, O God;
let all the peoples praise you!
[4] Let the nations be glad and sing for joy,
for you judge the peoples with equity
and guide the nations upon earth.
[5] Let the peoples praise you, O God;
let all the peoples praise you!
[6] The earth has yielded its increase;
God, our God, shall bless us.
[7] God shall bless us;
let all the ends of the earth fear him!

REVELATION 5:9-12

[9] And they sang a new song, saying, "Worthy are you to take
the scroll and to open its seals, for you were slain, and by your
blood you ransomed people for God from every tribe and
language and people and nation, [10] and you have made them
a kingdom and priests to our God, and they shall reign on the
earth." [11] Then I looked, and I heard around the throne and
the living creatures and the elders the voice of many angels,
numbering myriads of myriads and thousands of thousands,
[12] saying with a loud voice, "Worthy is the Lamb who was slain,
to receive power and wealth and wisdom and might and honor
and glory and blessing!"

+ **QUESTION 2:** In light of these verses, describe the relationship between worship and missions. Underline phrases in these passages that apply to this question.

QUESTION 3: In light of the above distinctions between missions and evangelism, are all Christians called to be missionaries? Are all Christians called to be missions-driven? Cite Scripture in your answer. List four ways that a passion for the majesty of Christ among all the nations of the world might express itself.

DAY 2—A PASSION FOR WORSHIP AND A PASSION FOR MISSIONS

Read from page 155 to the top of page 163 in *Don't Waste Your Life* and answer the following questions.

On page 158 John Piper quotes the following letter from Adoniram Judson to Ann Haseltine's father:

> I have now to ask, whether you can consent to part with your daughter early next spring, to see her no more in this world; whether you can consent to her departure, and her subjection to the hardships and sufferings of missionary life; whether you can consent to her exposure to the dangers of the ocean, to the fatal influence of the southern climate of India; to every kind of want and distress; to degradation, insult, persecution, and perhaps a violent death. Can you consent to all this, for the sake of him who left his heavenly home, and died for her and for you; for the sake of perishing, immortal souls; for the sake of Zion, and the glory of God? Can you consent to all this, in hope of soon meeting your daughter in the world of

> glory, with the crown of righteousness, brightened with acclamations of praise which shall redound to her Savior from heathens saved, through her means, from eternal woe and despair?

QUESTION 4: In Ann's case, was risk right (see Chapter 6)? If you were Ann's father, would you have let her go? If you were Ann, would you have gone? Give reasons for your answer.

QUESTION 5: Imagine once again that you are Ann's father. Imagine that another man has come to ask your daughter to go with him. He says, "If your daughter would come with me, she must deny herself, take up her cross, the instrument of her execution, and follow me to a hill where we both will be violently executed. She must lose her life in order to save it, and if she tries to save her life, she will surely lose it" (see Mark 8:34-38 and Galatians 2:19-20). How would you respond to this man? Is your answer to Question 4 different than your answer to Question 5? If so, why?

Read the following quote from John Piper's book on world missions, *Let the Nations Be Glad*, and answer the question that follows.

> Missions is not the ultimate goal of the church. Worship is. Missions exists because worship doesn't. Worship is ultimate, not missions, because God is ultimate, not man. When this age is over, and the countless millions of the redeemed fall on their faces before the throne of God, missions will be no more. It is a temporary necessity. But worship abides forever.[3]

+ **QUESTION 6:** In light of this excerpt, what is the relationship between worship and missions? Is it possible to have a passion for the worship of God through Jesus Christ and not have a passion for missions among all the people of the world? Why or why not?

DAY 3—THE JOYFUL PARTNERSHIP OF GOERS AND SENDERS

Read from the top of page 163 to the middle of page 171 in *Don't Waste Your Life* and answer the following questions.

Study Isaiah 46:9-10, Philippians 2:9-11, and Matthew 24:14.

ISAIAH 46:9-10

9 *Remember the former things of old;*

for I am God, and there is no other;
I am God, and there is none like me,
[10] *declaring the end from the beginning*
and from ancient times things not yet done,
saying, "My counsel shall stand,
and I will accomplish all my purpose."

PHILIPPIANS 2:9-11

[9] *Therefore God has highly exalted him and bestowed on him*
the name that is above every name, [10] *so that at the name of*
Jesus every knee should bow, in heaven and on earth and under
the earth, [11] *and every tongue confess that Jesus Christ is Lord,*
to the glory of God the Father.

MATTHEW 24:14

And this gospel of the kingdom will be proclaimed throughout the whole world as a testimony to all nations, and then the end will come.

+ **QUESTION 7:** How are these passages related to world missions? Underline the relevant portions in each passage. How do these passages provide a rock-solid foundation for the completion of the missionary task by the church?

QUESTION 8: In this section John Piper recounts a portion of the history of world missions in the last century. He highlights what he calls "the joyful partnership." What is this "joyful partnership"? What is your role in this partnership? What is the main point that you think John Piper wants us to draw out of this history lesson?

DAY 4—GOD'S CALL TO THIS GENERATION

Read from the middle of page 171 to page 179 in *Don't Waste Your Life* and answer the following questions.

+ QUESTION 9: In this section John Piper notes that "a passion for missions was not only the way to save the world, but also to save the church" (page 171). From what does the church need saving? How does a passion for missions serve to rescue us from this great danger? What evidence does John Piper supply to show that this is a very real danger for the church today?

On page 177 John Piper says the following:

> He [Christ] owns this world, and the allegiance of every person is his right. Every soul and every state is his. Abraham Kuyper put it memorably: "There is not a square inch in the whole domain of human existence over which Christ, who is Sovereign over all, does not cry: 'Mine!'"

QUESTION 10: What areas of life do people often try to keep Christ out of? What areas of life do you try to keep separate from Christ? Can you think of any Scripture verses that would support John Piper's claim in the quotation above?

DAY 5—REVIEW AND APPLICATION

Review your answers from the previous four days and any parts of *Don't Waste Your Life* that you want and then answer the following questions.

+ **QUESTION 11:** What was the most meaningful part of this chapter for you? Was there a sentence, concept, or idea that really struck you? Why? Record your thoughts in the space below.

On pages 174-175 John Piper says the following:

> There is a call on this generation to obey the risen Christ and make disciples of all the unreached peoples of the world. I am praying that God will raise up hundreds of thousands of young people and "finishers" (people finishing one career and ready to pursue a second in Christian ministry). I pray that this divine

> call will rise in your heart with joy and not guilt. I pray that it will be confirmed with the necessary gifts, and a compelling desire, and the confirmation of your church, and the tokens of providence. Fan into flame every flicker of desire by reading biographies, and meditating on Scripture, and studying the unreached peoples, and praying for passion, and conversing with mission veterans. Don't run from the call. Pursue it.

Later, on page 177, he encourages people to "stop and go away for a few days with a Bible and notepad; and pray and think about how your particular time and place in life fits into the great purpose of God to make the nations glad in him."

✦ **QUESTION 12:** In the quotation above, John Piper lists four things that he hopes will confirm any rising call in your heart to missions. What are they? Do you find any of these confirmations in your own life? If so, describe them below. Might it be possible for you to take a weekend and consider the exhortation from page 177? If so, write down the weekend you plan to do so. Be sure to tell your group so they can be praying for you.

FURTHER UP AND FURTHER IN

Study Revelation 5:9-10 and Revelation 7:9-10.

REVELATION 5:9-10

> [9] *And they sang a new song, saying, "Worthy are you to take*
> *the scroll and to open its seals, for you were slain, and by your*
> *blood you ransomed people for God from every tribe and*
> *language and people and nation,* [10] *and you have made them*
> *a kingdom and priests to our God, and they shall reign on the*
> *earth."*

REVELATION 7:9-10

> [9] *After this I looked, and behold, a great multitude that no one*
> *could number, from every nation, from all tribes and peoples*
> *and languages, standing before the throne and before the Lamb,*
> *clothed in white robes, with palm branches in their hands,*
> [10] *and crying out with a loud voice, "Salvation belongs to our*
> *God who sits on the throne, and to the Lamb!"*

QUESTION 13: What are the common themes in these passages? Underline the relevant phrases. In light of these themes, what conclusion could you draw about the relationship between the cross, where the blood of the Lamb was shed, and the population of heaven at the end of time? Did the cross succeed?

Study Romans 15:8-9 and Genesis 12:1-3.

ROMANS 15:8-9

[8] *For I tell you that Christ became a servant to the circumcised to show God's truthfulness, in order to confirm the promises given to the patriarchs,* [9] *and in order that the Gentiles might glorify God for his mercy.*

GENESIS 12:1-3

[1] *Now the* LORD *said to Abram, "Go from your country and your kindred and your father's house to the land that I will show you.* [2] *And I will make of you a great nation, and I will bless you and make your name great, so that you will be a blessing.* [3] *I will bless those who bless you, and him who dishonors you I will curse, and in you all the families of the earth shall be blessed."*

QUESTION 14: Romans 15:8-9 gives three purposes for why Jesus became a Jew ("a servant to the circumcised"). What are these three purposes? How does the promise to Abraham the patriarch in Genesis 12 explain Romans 15:8-9? Underline the relevant portions of the texts. In light of these verses, was Jesus motivated by zeal for God's glory or by a servant-heart of mercy for the nations when he came to earth?

In his book *Let the Nations Be Glad*, John Piper says the following about prayer and missions:

> Probably the number one reason prayer malfunctions in the hands of believers is that we try to turn a wartime walkie-talkie into a domestic intercom. Until you know that life is war, you cannot know what prayer is for. Prayer is for the accomplishment of a wartime mission. It is as though the field commander (Jesus) called in the troops, gave them a crucial mission (go and bear fruit), handed each of them a personal transmitter coded to the frequency of the General's headquarters, and said, "Comrades, the General has a mission for you. He aims to see it accomplished. And to that end he has authorized me to give each of you personal access to him through these transmitters. If you stay true to his mission and seek his victory first, he will always be as close as your transmitter, to give tactical advice and to send air cover when you need it."
>
> But what have millions of Christians done? We have stopped believing that we are in a war. No urgency, no watching, no vigilance. No strategic planning. Just easy peace and prosperity. And what did we do with the walkie-talkie? We tried to rig it up as an intercom in our houses and cabins and boats and cars—not to call in firepower for conflict with a mortal enemy but to ask for more comforts in the den.[4]

QUESTION 15: Do you think this is an accurate analogy about prayer and missions? Do you view prayer more as a wartime walkie-talkie or as a domestic intercom? Write two short prayers, one that views prayer as a wartime walkie-talkie and one that views it as a domestic intercom.

GROUP ACTIVITY

Complete this section during the group time each week.

Complete the following activity.

› Divide into groups of two or three.

› In your groups, discuss any current ideas you have about increasing your involvement in world missions.

› Pray that everyone in the group would grow in their desire to make much of Christ among all the nations of the world. Pray for the specific ideas that God is stirring in each person.

GETTING PRACTICAL

A suggested activity to do in the future: Look for an opportunity to engage with people from another country. If there is a university near you, seek out international students there. Perhaps you could find a program where you could help them to learn English and could learn about their culture.

NOTES

1. Excerpt taken from *Let the Nations Be Glad*, page 208.
2. Definitions taken from Stephen Hawthorne, *Perspectives on the World Christian Movement Study Guide* (Bletchley, UK: Paternoster, 1999), page 81.
3. Excerpt taken from *Let the Nations Be Glad*, page 17.
4. Excerpt taken from *Let the Nations Be Glad*, page 49.

LESSON 10

REVIEW AND CONCLUSION

LESSON OBJECTIVES

It is our prayer that after you have finished this lesson . . .

- You will be able to summarize and synthesize what you've learned.
- You will hear what others in your group have learned.
- You will share with others about how you aim to not waste your life.

WHAT HAVE YOU LEARNED?

There are no study questions to answer in preparation for this lesson. Instead, spend your time writing a few paragraphs that explain what you've learned in this group study. To help you do this, you may choose to review the notes you've taken in the previous lessons. Be sure to note any Scripture passages that have made an impact on you. Perhaps spend some time praying and evaluating your current life trajectory and what God might be calling you to do in the future. Then, after you've written down what you've learned, write down some questions that still remain in your mind about anything addressed in these lessons. Be prepared to share these reflections and questions with the group.

LEADER'S GUIDE

IT IS CRUCIAL THAT YOU, as the leader and facilitator of this group study, are completely familiar with this study guide. Therefore, it is our strong recommendation that you

(1) read and understand the Introduction,
(2) browse each lesson, surveying its format and content,
(3) read the entire Leader's Guide *before* you begin the group study and distribute the books and study guides.
(4) If you are using the *Don't Waste Your Life* DVD, preview the session(s) that correspond(s) to the chapter(s) you will be discussing.

BEFORE LESSON 1

Before the first lesson, you will need to count how many participants you will have in your group study. *Each participant will need his or her own study guide!* Each participant will also need his or her own copy of *Don't Waste Your Life*, although couples or families could share a copy of the book. Be sure to order enough study guides. You will distribute these study guides during the first lesson.

DURING LESSON 1

Each lesson is designed for a one-hour group session. Lessons 2-10 require preparatory work from the participant before the group session. Lesson 1, however, requires no preparation on the part of the participant.

The following schedule is how we suggest that you use the first hour of your group study.

INTRODUCTION TO THE STUDY GUIDE (10 MINUTES)

Introduce this study guide and *Don't Waste Your Life*. Explain to the group why you chose to lead the group study using these resources. Inform your group of the commitment that this study will require and encourage them to commit to doing the work. Then pray for your ten-week study, asking God for transforming and empowering grace. When you've finished praying, distribute one study guide to each participant. You may read the Introduction aloud if you want, or you may immediately turn the group to Lesson 1.

PERSONAL INTRODUCTIONS (20 MINUTES)

Since group discussion is an essential and primary activity in this guided study, it is vital that each participant feels welcomed and free to speak. Ideally, each week *every* participant will contribute to the discussion in some way. Therefore, during these twenty minutes have each participant introduce himself or herself. Use the questions listed in the section entitled "About Yourself" or ask questions of your own choosing. Try to be warm and inviting in your demeanor.

DISCUSSION (30 MINUTES)

As a group, work through the three questions in the "Preview of *Don't Waste Your Life*" section in Lesson 1. The purpose of this time is to allow the participants to begin to reflect on what they consider to be a meaningful life. It is also meant to expose the participants to *Don't Waste Your Life*. Be sure to examine the Table of Contents. Have one person read the Preface aloud to the group.

BEFORE LESSONS 2-9

As the group leader, you should do all the preparation for each lesson that is required of the group participants: you must complete the reading and thoughtfully answer the twelve study questions. Furthermore, it is *highly* recommended that you complete the entire "Further Up and Further In" section each week. This is not required of the group participants, but it will enrich your preparation and will enable you to guide and shape the conversation more effectively.

As the leader of the group, you may want to supplement or modify the study questions or the group activity. Please remember that *this study guide is a resource*—any additions or changes that tailor the study to your particular group are encouraged. This study guide should function as a helpful *tool*. As the group leader, your own discernment, creativity, and effort are invaluable, and you should adapt the material as you see fit, if you so desire.[1]

DURING LESSONS 2-9

Again, let it be said that during Lessons 2-9 you may use the group time in whatever way you desire. The following schedule, however, is what we recommend.

VIDEO (15 MINUTES)

DISCUSSION (40 MINUTES)

Open your time with prayer. Remember that the tone of your prayer will likely be impressed upon the group participants. If your prayer is sober and heart-felt, the group participants will be serious about prayer; if your prayer is hasty, sloppy, or a token gesture, the group participants will likely share this same approach toward prayer. So model the kind of praying that you desire the participants to imitate.

After praying, review the homework that the participants completed. How did they answer the questions? Which questions did they find to be the most interesting or the most confusing? What observations or insights can they share with the group? If you would like to consult some tips for leading productive discussion, please turn to Appendix B.

Questions marked with a cross (+) are questions that we deem to be particularly significant. You may choose to focus on these questions or, if there were other questions or parts of the chapter that you feel would be more helpful, spend time reviewing those.

Make sure that you point the participants again and again to the Bible as the source and foundation for the truth. Also, it is important that you encourage the participants to apply the things that they are learning to their lives. It is not enough to merely review the answers they have written. Push for practical, specific application. Model this yourself in the way that you discuss what God is teaching you through this study.

GROUP ACTIVITY (15 MINUTES)

At the end of each lesson there is a group activity. The purpose of these activities is to reinforce some of the truths learned during the week. As the group leader, you may decide that it is more helpful to spend more time discussing and thinking through the answers to the questions rather than completing the group activity. Again, this study guide is only a resource. Use your time together in the way that you feel will be most spiritually fruitful.

CONCLUSION (5 MINUTES)

Close the time by briefly reviewing the key concepts you have learned. Remind everyone of the "Getting Practical" activity, and urge them to do this or some similar activity during the upcoming week. If possible, you might want to set aside a time to do some of these practical activities as a group. We also encourage you to think of other activities that the participants could do individually or as a group in order to apply what you've been learning. Pray and dismiss.

BEFORE LESSON 10

It is important to encourage the group participants to thoughtfully complete the preparatory work for Lesson 10. This assignment invites the participants to reflect on what they have learned and to record what remaining questions they still have. As the group leader, this would be a helpful assignment for you to complete as well. In addition, you may want to write down the key concepts from *Don't Waste Your Life* that you want the group participants to remember as they finish this study. Make copies of your reflections to distribute to the group if you think that is appropriate.

DURING LESSON 10

The entirety of the group time during this last lesson should be concentrated on reviewing and synthesizing what was learned. If you are using the DVD, feel free to incorporate the DVD session anytime during the lesson. Encourage each participant to share some of what he or she has written. You may choose to do this in smaller groups if you want. Attempt to answer any remaining questions they might have.

To conclude this last lesson, you might want to spend extended time in prayer. If appropriate, ask for prayer requests relating to what the participants have learned in these ten weeks, and bring these requests to God.

It would be fitting and beneficial for you, as the group leader, to give a final charge or word of exhortation to end your group study. Speak from your heart and out of the overflow of joy that you have in God.

To every group leader who chooses to use this study guide, please receive our blessing:

> *The* LORD *bless you and keep you;*
> *the* LORD *make his face to shine upon you and be gracious to you;*
> *the* LORD *lift up his countenance upon you and give you peace.*
>
> NUMBERS 6:24-26

NOTES

1. Make special note of the Special Assignment that is given at the end of Lesson 6. This assignment should be completed before students come to the group to discuss Lesson 7. Participants will discuss this assignment during the Group Activity in Lesson 7. The Weekly Activity Log can be found in Appendix C.

APPENDIX A

A FIVE-SESSION INTENSIVE OPTION

WE UNDERSTAND THAT some circumstances may prohibit a group from devoting ten sessions to this study. In view of this, we have designed a five-session intensive option for groups that need to complete the material in less time. Here is our suggestion for how to complete the material in five weeks:

Week 1—Introduction (Lesson 1)
Week 2—Lessons 2 and 3 (Chapters 1 and 2)
Week 3—Lessons 4 and 5 (Chapters 3 and 4)
Week 4—Lessons 6 and 7 (Chapters 5, 6, and 7)[1]
Week 5—Lessons 8 and 9 (Chapters 8 and 9)

Notice that we have not included Lesson 10 in the intensive option. Moreover, because each participant is required to complete two lessons per week, it will be necessary to combine the number of "days" within each lesson so that all of the material is covered. Thus, for example, during Week 2 in the intensive option each participant will complete

- Lesson 1, Days 1 and 2, on the first day;
- Lesson 1, Days 3 and 4, on the second day;
- Lesson 1, Day 5 and Lesson 2, Day 1, on the third day;
- Lesson 2, Days 2 and 3, on the fourth day;
- Lesson 2, Days 4 and 5, on the fifth day.

Because of the amount of material, we recommend that students focus on questions marked with a cross (✚) first, and then, if time permits, complete the rest of the questions. Because participants will read the chapters and complete the lessons at varying speeds, we recommend that the leader of the study focus most of the attention during the group discussion on the questions marked with a cross.

NOTES

1. If you want to include the Weekly Activity Log (Appendix C) in Week 4 of the intensive option, then the group participants will need to complete this log after Week 3.

APPENDIX B

LEADING PRODUCTIVE DISCUSSIONS

Note: This material has been adapted from curricula produced by The Bethlehem Institute (TBI), a ministry of Bethlehem Baptist Church. It is used by permission.

IT IS OUR CONVICTION THAT the best group leaders foster an environment in their group that engages the participants. People of all ages learn by solving problems or by working through things that provoke curiosity or concern. Therefore, we discourage you from ever "lecturing" for the entire lesson. Although group leaders constantly shape conversation, clarifying and correcting as needed, they will probably not talk for the majority of the lesson. This study guide is meant to facilitate an investigation into biblical truth—an investigation that is shared by the group leader and the participants. Therefore, we encourage you to adopt the posture of a fellow-learner who invites participation from everyone in the group.

It might surprise you how eager people can be to share what they have learned in preparing for each lesson. Therefore, you should invite participation by asking your group participants to share their discoveries. Here are some of our tips on facilitating discussion that is engaging and helpful:

› Don't be uncomfortable with silence initially. Once the first participant shares his or her response, others will be likely to join in. But if you cut the silence short by prompting them, they are more likely to wait for you to prompt them every time.

- Affirm every answer, if possible, and draw out the participants by asking for clarification. Your aim is to make them feel comfortable sharing their ideas and learning; so be extremely hesitant to shut down a participant's contribution or to trump it with your own. This does not mean, however, that you shouldn't correct false ideas—but do it in a spirit of gentleness and love.
- Don't allow a single participant, or group of participants, to dominate the discussion. Involve everyone, if possible, and intentionally invite participation from those who are more reserved or hesitant.
- Labor to show the significance of their study. Emphasize the things that the participants could not have learned without doing the homework.
- Avoid talking too much. The group leader should not monopolize the discussion but rather guide and shape it. If the group leader does the majority of the talking, the participants will be less likely to interact and engage, and therefore they will not learn as much. Avoid constantly adding the "definitive last word."
- The group leader should feel the freedom to linger on a topic or question if the group demonstrates interest. The group leader should also pursue digressions that are helpful and relevant. There is a balance to this, however: the group leader *should* attempt to cover the material. So avoid the extreme of constantly wandering off topic, but also avoid the extreme of limiting the conversation in a way that squelches curiosity or learning.
- The group leader's passion, or lack of it, is infectious. Therefore, if you demonstrate little enthusiasm for the material, it is almost inevitable that your participants will likewise be bored. But if you have a genuine excitement for what you are studying, and if you truly think Bible study is worthwhile, your group will be impacted

positively. Therefore, it is our recommendation that before you come to the group you spend enough time working through the homework and praying so you can overflow with genuine enthusiasm for the Bible and for God in your group. This point cannot be stressed enough. Delight yourself in God and in his Word!

APPENDIX C: WEEKLY ACTIVITY LOG

ACTIVITIES	# OF MINUTES SPENT		
1) Eating:			
2) Sleeping:			
3) Work, school, homework, household chores:			
4) Driving:			
5) Exercising:			
6) Reading:			
7) Listening to music:			
8) Watching TV:			
9) Spare computer time (Internet, video games, etc.):			
10) Talking on the phone:			
11) Shopping:			
12) Time spent with friends, family:			
13) Time spent with unbelievers:			
14) Time spent alone:			
15) Other habitual activities (list):			
	SUNDAY	MONDAY	TUESDAY

Please note: If you engaged in two activities simultaneously, record the number of minutes spent in each box. So, for example, if you ate dinner and watched TV at the same time on Monday, record the number of minutes you spent in box #1 **AND** box #8 of the Monday column.

WEDNESDAY	THURSDAY	FRIDAY	SATURDAY	TOTALS	% OF WEEK (10,080 MIN./ WEEK)

APPENDIX D:

LIST OF HELPFUL RESOURCES[1]

RESOURCES FOR MAKING MUCH OF CHRIST FROM 8 TO 5

Business for the Glory of God: The Bible's Teaching on the Moral Goodness of Business by Wayne Grudem

Callings: Twenty Centuries of Christian Wisdom on Vocation, edited by William Placher

God at Work: Your Christian Vocation in All of Life by Gene Edward Veith, Jr.

Luther on Vocation by Gustaf Wingren

Spiritual Leadership: Moving People to God's Agenda by Henry and Richard Blackaby

The Book on Leadership by John MacArthur

The Pursuit of Excellence by Ted Engstrom

The Making of a Mentor: Nine Essential Characteristics of Influential Christian Leaders by Ted Engstrom and Ron Jenson

RESOURCES FOR GETTING INVOLVED IN GOD'S GLOBAL PURPOSE

A History of Christian Missions by Stephen Neill

Anointed for Business by Ed Silvoso

Great Commission Companies: The Emerging Role of Business in Missions by Steven Rundle and Tom Steffen

Let the Nations Be Glad by John Piper

Operation World: When We Pray God Works by Patrick Johnstone and others

The Church Is Bigger Than You Think by Patrick Johnstone

Caleb Project website: www.calebproject.org

Evangelical Missions Quarterly: http://bgc.gospelcom.net/emis/

Finishers Project: www.finishers.org/

Joshua Project website: www.joshuaproject.net

U.S. Center for World Missions website: www.uscwm.org

Voice of the Martyrs: http://www.persecution.com/

NOTES

1. Desiring God does not necessarily endorse specific authors or what they write, so with all things please remember to read with biblical discernment. Take the good; leave the bad. Furthermore, a link to a document or site other than those within the Desiring God domain does not necessarily imply that Desiring God endorses the organization(s) or person(s) providing them, agrees with the ideas expressed, or attests to the correctness, factuality, appropriateness, or legality of the contents.

desiringGod

If you would like to explore further the vision of God and life presented in this book, we at Desiring God would love to serve you. We have thousands of resources to help you grow in your passion for Jesus Christ and help you spread that passion to others. At our website, www.desiringGod.org, you'll find almost everything John Piper has written and preached, including more than forty books. We've made over thirty years of his sermons available free online for you to read, listen to, download, and in some cases watch.

In addition, you can access hundreds of articles, find out where John Piper is speaking, learn about our conferences, and browse our online store. John Piper receives no royalties from the books he writes and no compensation from Desiring God. The funds are all reinvested into our gospel-spreading efforts. Desiring God also has a whatever-you-can-afford policy, designed for individuals with limited discretionary funds. If you'd like more information about this policy, please contact us at the address or phone number below. We exist to help you treasure Jesus Christ and his gospel above all things because he is most glorified in you when you are most satisfied in him. Let us know how we can serve you!

Desiring God
Post Office Box 2901 Minneapolis, Minnesota 55402
888.346.4700 mail@desiringGod.org

Personal Notes

Personal Notes

Personal Notes

Personal Notes